Creating a Cottage Garden

Creating a Cottage Garden

in North America

Stephen Westcott-Gratton

photographs by Paddy Wales

FULCRUM PUBLISHING

A DENISE SCHON BOOK

To my parents

Ruth and Peter

with love

A Denise Schon Book

Copyright © 2000 Denise Schon Books Inc.
Text copyright © 2000 Stephen Westcott-Gratton
Photographs copyright © 2000 Paddy Wales

Library of Congress Cataloging-in-Publication Data

Westcott-Gratton, Stephen.
Creating a cottage garden in North America / Stephen Westcott-Gratton.
   p. cm.
ISBN 1-55591-441-1 (hc)
1. Cottage gardens – North America.
2. Cottage gardening – North America. I. Title

SB454.3.C67W47 2000
635—dc21
99-055327

Fulcrum Publishing
16100 Table Mountain Parkway, Suite 300
Golden, Colorado 80403
(800) 992-2908 • (303) 277-1623
www.fulcrum-books.com

Published in Canada by Raincoast Books

Produced by: Denise Schon Books Inc.
Text design: Linda Gustafson/Counterpunch
Editorial: Wendy Thomas
Index: Barbara Schon
Color separation: Quadratone Graphics

Printed in Hong Kong

0 9 8 7 6 5 4 3 2 1

PHOTOGRAPHS
A big thank you to Stephanie Etches and Gerald Obre for taking such good care of me on my visits to the West Coast.

   Many, many thanks to the great gardeners and friends who gave Paddy and me access to their glorious gardens. Judith Adam, pp. 44, 49; Therese D'Monte, pp. 38, 152; Ellen and Robert Eisenberg, pp. 14, 41, 46, 149, 151; Merike Lugus and Rod Anderson, p. 13; Phoebe Noble and Sandra Holloway, pp. 17, 140, 147; Gene Simon, pp. 9, 29; Alice and Walter Wikaruk, p. 32; Andrew Yeoman and Noel Richardson, pp. 82, 135, back cover.

   In case you're interested, my garden appears on pp. 10, 19, 35, 61, 117. SWG

We thank Spadina House for allowing us access to their gardens: pp. 6, 8, 100, 136, 155.

Contents

CHAPTER ONE

What Is a Cottage Garden?

THE CONCEPT OF AN English cottage garden in North America may seem slightly incongruous — after all, we don't have the thatched-roof cottages and mossy stone walls that many of us automatically associate with these traditional gardens. But other than climate, those are our only limitations, and they certainly haven't stopped English gardeners in modern townhouses from recreating this venerable style on whatever sort of real estate they find themselves. The same then is equally true for North Americans.

You'll find a number of definitions for "the cottage garden style." This is due to the fact that the style is as organic as the gardens themselves and is always shifting and changing, to adapt itself to new influences and circumstances. The earliest cottage gardens were little more than pig pens, with plants playing a singularly second fiddle to any livestock, often being used as fodder for animals rather than for people. Contrast that early reality with some of the very idealized Victorian paintings, still celebrated in spite of their unrealistic depictions of apple-cheeked peasants, ubiquitous puffy white clouds racing across a cobalt blue sky, and a glut of perpetually flowering plants. In truth, the genuine cottage garden lies somewhere between the two.

The cottage garden is a profusion of flowering plants and produce, all growing together in a glorious jumble. This arrangement suits our needs better than we might at first think, since English cottages had about the same amount of garden space as do modern homes in many urban centers. The push is once again on to make the most of every inch. Different needs and interests will dictate the individual flavor of present-day cottage gardens. Some people will concentrate primarily on fruit or vegetables, with flowers playing a supporting role only, while

A casual layout brimming with a wide variety of plant material is key to a healthy, abundant cottage garden.

Nurturing a cosmopolitan mixture of flowers, herbs and vegetables

together in one space is a basic tenet of the cottage garden style.

Dense planting patterns outcompete annual weed seedlings

and reduce the need for staking.

others will strive for a riot of color, with the occasional tomato or green pea struggling up through the clematis.

With luck, most of the plants engaged in "the struggle" will only be weeds. That's because to achieve the abundant look, plants have to be placed very close to one another, and therein lies the secret of the cottage garden: Dense planting will go a long way in keeping weeds out of your garden, since aggressive aliens (as the eco-warriors like to refer to them) will soon discover there's no room at the inn. Established plants will usually outcompete weed

seedlings for sunlight, moisture, and nutrients. Add some mulch to the equation and they won't stand a chance. Another advantage of planting densely is that the flowers will tend to support each other like teenagers at a jam-packed midnight rave, reducing the need for staking.

The most important thing to remember about cottage gardens is that they are very unpretentious, catholic spaces, easily achievable, and certainly within everyone's grasp. They don't require big budgets since additional structures such as trellises or arbors are kept to a minimum and most of the plants can be grown inexpensively from seed. You won't need to employ a landscape architect, because that will be your job. You won't need to cut the grass every Saturday morning, because there won't be much. For at least half the year you won't have to pay high prices for organically grown fruit, herbs, and vegetables, because you'll have your own. Best of all, you won't have to attend night classes on garden design, because there aren't any. Naturally, you'll look for pleasing color, height and texture combinations, but symmetry and balance are not paramount considerations.

The most successful cottage gardens are simple ones that work directly with nature. These are the gardens that are the healthiest and therefore the loveliest. Authentic cottage gardens were not contrived affairs, being the result of country artisans who were short on free time and whose aesthetic senses were closely linked to the countryside. It is this lack of sophistication that makes these plots tick, and the surest way to ruin a cottage garden is to install an elaborate fountain or to try to "tidy things up" with boxwood hedging. Neatness has been thrown on the sacrificial altar in favor of unabashed exuberance and bounty.

The result of all this freedom and profusion is a

Starting from Scratch

In many respects, creating a cottage garden where nothing exists is easier than converting an established garden. There are no mature trees to contend with, nor are there weedy, deep-rooted groundcovers or old paving to be removed — in fact, you have before you a clean, blank canvas. Use the following steps to help you get started planning your new, old-fashioned cottage garden.

1. Before you do anything else, have a good look at the condition of your soil. Now is the time to test your soil for pH, organic matter and nutrient levels.

2. Once you're satisfied that your soil is in good shape, one of the first things you will want to contemplate are trees. These large, permanent structures require a good deal of forethought — never be hasty when deciding on a tree species. If your garden space is small and your house is tall and narrow, you will want to consider upright "fastigiate" tree forms such as the 'Purple Fountain' beech (*Fagus sylvatica* 'Purple Fountain'). If you live in a bungalow on a larger lot, small to medium-sized fruit and nut trees will likely look more appropriate. You may want to include some evergreens, but bear in mind that small trees like the corkscrew hazel (*Corylus avellana* 'Contorta') and many of the dogwoods (*Cornus* spp.) provide winter interest in spite of their deciduous constitutions. A list of native trees appropriate to cottage gardens appears on page 39.

3. The next thing to ponder is how you intend to enclose your garden perimeters. Some gardeners will opt for a fence, while others will prefer to use roses, shrubs and dwarf trees for this purpose. Refer to the list "Fruit and Nut Varieties Suitable for Informal Cottage Garden Hedges" on page 42, and the list of roses for hedging on page 44 to start you off on the right track.

4. The next order of business will be to start thinking about the placement of the flower beds, where the paths will be, and what they are to be constructed of. When thinking about the layout of the paths, don't forget about using vertical accents (trellises, arbors, archways) to frame views and add height to the garden.

5. As you are mapping out your garden, also be aware of the possibility of benches, birdbaths, sundials and other bits of "hardware." While these ornaments are likely still a few years down the road for you, it's never too soon to start thinking about their eventual placement.

6. Last, but by no means least, comes the seriously fun part — choosing the plants. If you're on a strict budget, remember that most cottage garden plants grow easily from seed, and if you possess even a little patience, you'll soon find yourself with plenty of plants for a fraction of the garden center price. Remember to leave plenty of "bare patches" for spring bulbs, to be followed by annual flowers, vegetables and herbs.

In a very dry, sunny section of my Toronto garden, I grow plants that tolerate or even enjoy these ascetic conditions. Selecting plant material that is appropriate to your individual microclimates is crucial if you are to achieve cottage-gardening success. The majority of the plants pictured here were grown from seed for a fraction of their garden center price tag.

What Is a Cottage Garden?

great deal of flexibility for the plants themselves, not to mention the gardeners. In formal gardens, spring bulbs must be ripped out in order to make way for bedding plants, reducing them to the status of pricey annuals. Strictly herbaceous borders heavily planted with perennials offer no extra nooks and crannies for vegetables or flowering annuals. Neither of these approaches is characteristic of the cottage garden.

The backbone of any garden is made up of static woody and perennial plant material, but the cottage garden should always have blank spaces available for successional planting. All this means is that as one crop is harvested, another takes its place. It's not that there are bare patches of soil waiting for attention, but that there is a natural rhythm to the garden: early spring daffodils will fade, and a quick crop of radishes will take their place. Once the radishes have been harvested, seedlings of an annual bush-type morning glory will take over, providing bloom until the first frosts. This technique has recently been referred to as "square foot gardening" — not a bad moniker, since it reminds us that every square foot of land is important and should be encouraged to produce to its full potential.

The idea of planting for a succession of crops was foremost in the English cottage gardener's mind, since arable land was often scarce and always precious. The same can be said for many of the pioneer style or dooryard gardens of the early North American settlers. While some of these gardens may be said to stem from the classic English cottage garden style, they were also influenced by the traditions of the settlers themselves, and usually reflected their country of origin, be it Dutch, Irish, Scandinavian or German. Because of this, these gardens must be considered offshoots rather than genuine successors to the cottage garden style.

This book will show you how to attain the classic English look using traditional plant material as well as other plants that are available to modern gardeners, many of them North American natives. (Check out the features in this chapter, "Starting from Scratch" and "Converting an Existing Garden"; the practical information you'll find there will help you as you put your cottage garden together.)

When we discuss "native plants" in the following pages, we are of course referring to North American natives and will use the ❀ symbol as a quick reference to remind you that they're indigenous to these shores. Often designating a plant as native is easy — take for example bloodroot (*Sanguinaria canadensis*). Not only is bloodroot the only species in its genus, but it is found growing wild only in the moist forests of eastern North America, so designating it as "native" is a clear-cut procedure. On the other hand, a gregarious plant like Jacob's ladder (*Polemonium caeruleum*) enjoys a much more cosmopolitan distribution and is found growing wild in northern and central Europe, northern Asia and western North America. Due to this wide natural distribution, Jacob's ladder must be considered a native of all three continents.

Some people get very hung up about what is genuinely native and what is not, so it's important to remember that plants have been travelling the globe for millennia, often without any sort of human interference. We should consider that any plant is fair game for the North American cottage garden providing it isn't invasive (like purple loosestrife — *Lythrum salicaria*) or destructive to local habitats.

To enhance your appreciation of the plants profiled throughout these pages, we will also look at their histories and the sometimes circuitous detours they took en route to our new North American cottage gardens. Knowing about the history of

Even a modest plant like the nasturtium (Tropaeolum majus)
can have a multitude of associations and uses for cottage gardeners.
Investigating the histories of the plants you cherish will enliven your
appreciation of them, alerting you to their foibles, while reminding
you of their merits.

particular plants will inspire you to experiment with plants that are new to you or to look with renewed interest at common plants such as morning glories and native plants.

We all choose the plants in our gardens for different reasons, and every plant has its own associations for each of us. Take the humble nasturtium (*Tropaeolum majus*), which has been a fixture in cottage gardens since the seventeenth century. Depending on your interests and background, you might grow it because you, like Lyle Lovett, know it's the birthday flower for your natal day: the first of November. Perhaps you're cultivating a patch of ground featuring the flowers of Peru, or maybe you're even Peruvian yourself, and remember it growing wild when you were young. Maybe you're experimenting with the genus as a whole and have a collection of several nasturtium species. Possibly your interest is more basic, and you want the colorful vitamin C-rich flowers as a peppery addition to salads, or the unripe seed heads for pickling instead of using costly capers. You may even be planting nasturtiums as an aphid trap, so that the pests will congregate on them rather than on your vegetables and roses, making their removal and destruction a much more efficient process. If you're up on your "language of flowers" and you love your country, you'll likely grow nasturtiums because they symbolize patriotism. If you have a Thomas Jefferson complex, you'll have to grow them once you discover that he had "35 little hills" of them at Monticello. Those of you with a herbal bent may want to grow them for their antibiotic constituents. Or maybe they were your grandmother's favorite flower. Perhaps, God forbid, you just like them for themselves.

Whatever the case, old-fashioned flowers (including native North American species) all have a story to tell, and all have unique qualities, much like the people who cultivate them. Their links to past generations — theirs and ours — make them all the more precious to us, and all the more worthy of space in our gardens. It also helps to put into perspective the brief span allotted to us, and reminds us that we alone are the stewards of these plants in our own generation. It's a daunting yet noble responsibility.

❧ Converting an Existing Garden

Many of the steps for transforming an existing garden (whatever the style) to a cottage garden are the same as when you start the process from scratch. The major difference between the two is that if you already have a garden, you also already have some permanent (and immovable) objects which need to be incorporated into the overall design.

1. The first obstacle usually comes in the form of mature trees. "Limbing up" or pruning out the lower branches will enhance air circulation and light levels on the ground, and planting species tolerant of dry shady conditions (see the suggestions on page 40) will mean that mature trees are no longer an impediment to the growth of a lush garden beneath their leafy canopies.

2. Other "immovable structures" may come in the form of garden sheds, garages, or decks, patios and verandas. Without a doubt, the easiest way to blend these structures into the cottage garden is to emphasize them, rather than trying to pretend they don't exist. Here's where you can allow yourself to go over the top, first with paints and stains to draw attention to the form of these structures, and then with plant material which can be festooned about wherever space allows.

3. The next stage will be to decide where the flower beds and paths are to be placed (See Starting from Scratch on page 9, Step 4). There will likely be grass that needs removing, and if this is the case, consider converting one section of the garden at a time — it will prove to be a more leisurely, enjoyable experience than if you try to do everything at once, ultimately becoming overwhelmed in the process (see pages 37–39).

Immovable structures like garages, verandas and sheds should be accentuated in the North American cottage garden — trying to hide them only serves to emphasize their presence. Here, artist Merike Lugus uses three shades of paint to frame a garden shed window and then softens it with plantings of (l to r) fragrant honeysuckle and lilies, juniper and wisteria.

4. Now it's time to assess the plant material you already have. "Do I need all these yews, or should I replace them with flowering or fruit-bearing shrubs?" "Rather than bare brick, would a wisteria look nice climbing up the house?" "Would the peonies look better in clusters of three or five, rather than plonked around the garden?" These are the kinds of questions you will need to address, and the final decision will reflect your own taste and style.

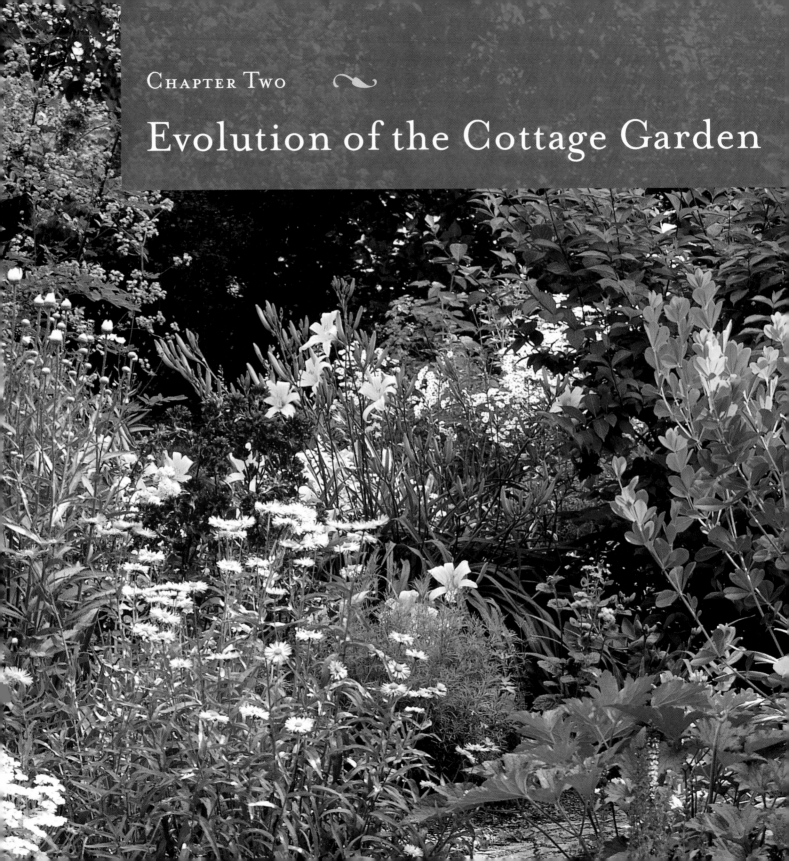

CHAPTER TWO

Evolution of the Cottage Garden

Before we look at the cottage garden in North America today, let's take a look back. It's important to have an understanding of the history of the cottage garden in England, and how it evolved, to get a sense of how to adapt it to our conditions and the contemporary landscape.

Ancient History

It may surprise many present-day gardeners that the native flora of Britain was not as extensive and varied as they might expect it to have been. During the Great Ice Age, Britain was scoured and scraped bare by glaciers not once, but seven or eight times. As long as the land bridge with Europe remained, plants and animals could migrate south to warmer regions during the coldest periods, and then re-colonize northern areas during the warmer interglacial reprieves. This is what occurred in species-rich areas like China and North America; there was always a permanent land route south, so that few species were lost even during the most frigid intervals. Once sea levels rose, however, and Britain became an island, no escape route was available, and many species like the alpine poppy (*Papaver alpinum*), which had previously been native to Britain, were lost forever.

The plant diversity of Britain was slowly restored as different peoples and cultures, beginning with the Celts and later the Angles, Jutes and Saxons, invaded the island. With them they brought the plants they needed for food and medicine. The Roman occupation in particular brought with it many important plants, including numerous vegetables, culinary herbs, and fruit that we now take for granted. It's difficult to decide whether these introductions that have

Unlike the cottage gardens of yesteryear, twenty-first-century enthusiasts have a bewildering number of plant varieties at their disposal.

been naturalizing across Britain for the last 2,000 years can strictly speaking be called native, but many of them very likely grew in Britain during inter-glacial periods when Britain was still connected to the European landmass. Certainly the importation of "exotic" plants to Britain has continued to some extent ever since, reaching its pinnacle in the last hundred years.

THE FIRST COTTAGE GARDENS

Our impression of what a cottage garden should look like is based more on recent images rather than on its true medieval origins and is influenced more by artists than by reality. The first cottagers were a miserable lot indeed. Their hovels had leaky thatched roofs, and the walls were constructed of wattle: interlaced twigs and branches, covered in mud or clay. If they were lucky enough to have some livestock, the chickens and pigs would share the dank family dwelling during the winter months, as much for the heat they gave off as for their own well-being. The stench must have been odious. Bee-keeping would have been attempted in most cottage gardens, since honey was still the only sweetener, sugar cane not yet having been discovered.

The plants that graced cottage gardens during this early period were grown exclusively for food, intended both for man and beast. Most cottagers were vegetarian by necessity rather than by choice. The wealthy classes ate hardly any vegetables at all and lived almost entirely on meat and other animal products such as cheese and eggs. The cottagers, on the other hand, were fortunate if they got a little

meat once a week and lived primarily on a soupy meatless stew called "pottage," a dreary concoction of any available vegetables combined with stock or water and seasoned with herbs. Interestingly, pro-tein-rich white beans (as in Boston baked) were raised and consumed in fairly large quantities and are mentioned several times in *The Forme of Cury*, a cookbook written in 1378. Simmered beans were combined with an almond mixture to which honey and raisins were added for sweetness. Other com-monly grown vegetables were leeks, onions, fennel, peas, turnips and cabbage. These must have been windy days indeed!

> ### ❧ Native Plants that Survived Britain's Last Ice Age (c. 10,000 BC)
>
> Cornflower – *Centauria cyanus* – Self-seeding annual
> Johnny-jump-up – *Viola tricolor* – Zones 3–8, Self-seeding short-lived perennial
> English holly – *Ilex aquifolium* – Zones 6–9, Evergreen shrub
> English ivy – *Hedera helix* – Zones 5–9, Clinging evergreen vine
> Jacob's ladder – *Polemonium caeruleum* – Zones 4–8, Perennial
> Meadow sweet – *Filipendula ulmaria* – Zones 3–8, Perennial
> Mountain avens – *Dryas octopetala* – Zones 3–6, Flowering sub-shrub
> Oregano (Wild marjoram) – *Origanum vulgare* – Zones 4–8, Perennial herb
> Purple mountain saxifrage – *Saxifraga oppositifolia* – Zones 2–6, Perennial
> Sea thrift – *Armeria maritima* – Zones 3–8, Perennial
> Self-heal – *Prunella vulgaris* – Zones 4–8, Perennial
> Water mint – *Mentha aquatica* – Zones 5–8, Semi-aquatic perennial herb
> Yellow water lily – *Nuphar lutea* – Zones 5–10, Aquatic perennial

Plants Brought to Britain by the Romans

Alexanders (wild) – *Smyrnium olusatrum* – Zones 5–9, Biennial or short-lived perennial vegetable

Common mallow – *Malva sylvestris* – Zones 4–8, Medicinal perennial

Cilantro (Coriander) – *Coriandrum sativum* – Annual culinary herb

Deadly nightshade – *Atropa belladonna* – Zones 5–8, Perennial medicinal

Dill – *Anethum graveolens* – Annual culinary herb

Fennel – *Foeniculum vulgare* – Zones 4–8, Perennial herb

Goutweed – *Aegopodium podagraria* – Zones 3–9, Medicinal perennial (invasive)

Henbane – *Hyoscyamus niger* – Medicinal annual (perennial in Zones 10–11)

Opium poppy – *Papaver somniferum* – Self-seeding medicinal annual

Scotch thistle – *Onopordum acanthium* – Zones 5–8, Medicinal biennial (and not Scottish at all!)

Fruit and Nuts Brought to Britain by the Romans

Common fig – *Ficus carica* – Zones 6–9, Deciduous fruit tree

Medlar – *Mespilus germanica* – Zones 6–9, Spreading deciduous fruit tree or large shrub

Mulberry (Black) – *Morus nigra* – Zones 5–9, Rounded deciduous fruit tree

Plum – *Prunus domestica* – Zones 3–8, Deciduous fruit tree

Walnut (English) – *Juglans regia* – Zones 4–8, Deciduous nut tree

Brought to Britain by the Romans, the springtime blooms of medlar (Mespilus germanica, hardy to zones 6 to 9) put our ubiquitous crabapples (Malus spp.) to shame. With 2 inch (5 cm) blossoms in shades of purest white to barely pink, the autumn fruits are no less dramatic, although the old English epithet of "open-arse" was more tactfully described by Shakespeare in Romeo and Juliet *as "open et cetera."*

⌘ Cowslip Wine

Here are two recipes for cowslip wine. The first is from the late seventeenth century, the second from the early twentieth century, and they are strikingly similar.

From Hartman's *Family Physitian*, 1696

Having boil'd your Water and Sugar together, pour it boiling hot upon your Cowslips beaten, stir them well together, and let them stand in a Vessel close cover'd till it be almost cold; then put into it the Yest beaten with the Juice of Lemons; let it stand for two days, then press it out with as much speed as you can, and put it into a Cask, and leave a little hole open, for the working; when it hath quite done working stop it up close for a Month or Six Weeks, then Bottle it. Cowslip wine is very Cordial, and a glass of it being drank at night Bedward, causes sleep and rest.

From *Mrs. Beeton's Cookery Book*, c. 1915

4 qt. cowslip flowers
3 lb. loaf sugar
4 qt. water
1 orange
1 lemon
¼ oz. dried yeast moistened with water
¼ pint brandy (optional)

Boil the sugar and water together for half an hour, skimming when necessary, and pour, quite boiling, over the finely-grated rind and juice of the orange and lemon. Let it cool, then put in the yeast and cowslip flowers, cover with a cloth, and allow it to remain undisturbed for 48 hours. Strain and pour into a clean dry cask, add the brandy, bung closely, let it remain for eight weeks, then draw it off into bottles. Cork securely, store in a cool, dry place for 3–4 weeks, and it will then be ready for use.

In addition to the widespread use of almonds in early medieval cooking, it's astonishing to learn that the other ingredient constantly required in surviving recipes is saffron. Saffron is, of course, just the stigmas of the autumn crocus (*Crocus sativa*), a small, late-season ornamental that was once widely cultivated in England, especially in the Essex area. Although we tend to associate this plant more with Spanish cooking than with English, it's a pity it isn't grown more widely in North America, since in many gardens the hardy autumn crocus is the last plant to be seen blooming in the fall before the well-known spring crocus takes over some months later. It's a genus capable of performing a seasonal *aloha* to perfection.

Living in rural areas as the cottagers did, there was also a good deal of fruit to be had from the hedgerows and fields. In season, blackberries, raspberries, currants, strawberries and tree fruit such as pears, apples and plums could often be culled from the wild, although it's amazing that winter scurvy wasn't more prevalent. Over the years, as a matter of convenience, cottagers began to collect specimens from the countryside and transplant them near their homes to facilitate easier harvest. It was at about this time, in the thirteenth to fifteenth centuries, that a greater number of flowering plants, valuable in their own right, but ornamental to boot, first made inroads into the cottage garden. Cowslips (*Primula veris*), for instance, would have been planted for the production of sweet cowslip wine in the spring, as would an increasing number of other wild flowers and herbs. Cowslips were used for a number of ailments, and needless to say, cowslip wine was the most popular way of ingesting them.

My appreciation for the small, airy flowers of vervain (Verbena officinalis) seems to increase each year. Providing a rigid, upright frame through which to view the background plantings, vervain prefers a lean soil that remains on the dry side. Other members of the **Verbena** family worthy of cottage garden culture are the showier native blue vervain (V. hastata) or V. bonariensis, a self-seeding tender perennial.

The Cottage in Transition

The cottage garden remained virtually unchanged until the 1530s, when the historic event most responsible for fostering the practice of planting herbs near the cottage came about. The catalyst was the dissolution of the monasteries by Henry VIII. Up until then, the peasants had depended on the monks and nuns for a sort of rudimentary nationalized health care system, based almost entirely on herbal medicine. Once the monasteries were dissolved, it's nearly certain that their adjacent gardens would have been plundered for the useful plants they contained, which would in turn have been transplanted nearer the cottages. Unfortunately, when the clerics left, so did much of their knowledge of how the herbs should be used, and it's at this point that many superstitions also made their way into the practice of country medicine. Plants like vervain (*Verbena officinalis*) and Johnny-jump-up (*Viola tricolor*) became associated with witches and sorcerers, and were widely used in love potions and amulets; yarrow (*Achillea millefolium*), by contrast, was useful for breaking spells. At the same time, knowledge of the use of poisons such as monkshood (*Aconitum napellus*), henbane (*Hyoscyamus niger*) and poison hemlock (*Conium maculatum*) became more widespread.

The fortunes of cottage gardeners during the Elizabethan age were as intimately tied to politics, and thus commerce, as they were to the weather. Luckily, the weather was good during most of Elizabeth I's rule, and so was commerce. The expansion of the navy had begun during her father's time, but it was in Elizabeth's reign that England could first be said to "rule the waves," despite an embargo by the Spanish and Portuguese. As is always the case, some of the new prosperity slowly trickled down to the peasant classes, improving their lot substantially for the first time in several hundred years. For that, they could thank Elizabeth's unscrupulous pirates, who captured masses of Spanish gold, which in turn had been unceremoniously stolen from the native peoples of this continent. At the same time, new plants began to appear from the New World that changed the face of European gardens forever.

There is no doubt that as soon as these plants from the New World were made available to cottagers — usually as cuttings or seeds from the manor house — they immediately began to grow and experiment with them. Early cottage gardeners had no concept of growing traditional cottage garden plants. They were eager to try everything, much like novice gardeners who get their hands on a really good plant catalog for the first time. If there was garden space available, any fresh introduction was fair game.

Toward the end of the sixteenth century, French Huguenots arrived in England and began working as weavers and lace-makers from their cottages. With them they brought arguably the loveliest of all spring flowers, the auricula (*Primula auricula*). While auriculas aren't fussy plants, having as they do an alpine constitution, they were typically grown in pots in a sheltered "auricula theater," a roofed wooden staging that was usually painted black to show off the charming velvety blooms and mealy foliage, while protecting the plants from direct sunlight and rain. Inflicting this sort of unnatural treatment on any plant is enough to send shivers down the spine, but it did lead to the breeding of some exquisite cultivars. Fortunately for us, auricula stages are a thing of the past, and these classic cottage garden plants can once again reside in the open borders.

In the late sixteenth century, the breeding of auriculas led to another craze for what was known as "florists' flowers." The florists' movement, originally confined to cottagers working from their homes, fostered many of the horticultural societies and clubs that exist to this day. The florists had nothing to do with flower arranging — it was simply the name that was given to cottagers who grew and hybridized these specialty plants. By the eighteenth century, florists' flowers were reckoned to include eight species, singled out for this unusual attention: anemone, auricula, carnation, hyacinth, pinks, polyanthus, ranunculus and tulip. These plants were enthusiastically grown for exhibition (another practice that I disapprove of — it all seems so arbitrary), but it did lead to the active dissemination of information and, more importantly, the sharing of plant material.

Over the next hundred and fifty years or so, cottagers saw their fortunes rise and fall in cycles. It's horrifying to remember that these humble habitats were not freehold. The landlord was capable of turning his workers out of their homes at a moment's notice, and indeed this happened fairly regularly. Some landlords rebuilt villages on other sites and in fact improved the cottager's standard of living, but frequently the tenants were left to fend for themselves.

Gradually reforms were introduced, and in 1846, nine years into Victoria's reign, the Corn Laws were repealed. These laws, introduced in 1804, had forbidden the importation of foreign grain, keeping the English prices high, but leading to much starvation among the poorer classes who could no longer afford to buy bread.

Philanthropic souls like John Loudon, an architect and gardening journalist, brought the plight of cottagers to the public's attention, and slowly things began to improve. Cottage gardens were enlarged, and greater self-sufficiency was encouraged. Allotments outside the villages that were intended to act as supplementary kitchen gardens were established for cottagers. Allotments were considered to be the husband's domain, while the housewives were responsible for the gardens around the home. With the advent of allotments in the mid-nineteenth century, cottage gardens for the first time had additional space for growing flowers since the bulk of food production had been moved elsewhere.

❧ John Gerard (1545–1612)

The name of Gerard appears again and again in gardening texts and the reason is simple. Gerard's *Herball* represents one of the first, and certainly one of the finest, books of its kind in the English language, and for generations after his death it remained required reading for aspiring surgeons, herbalists and gardeners alike.

For the 20 years prior to the publication of his *Herball* (in December 1597), Gerard worked as superintendent-of-gardens at Lord Burleigh's London estate in the Strand. He also kept a garden of his own, which boasted over 1,000 different species — a remarkable achievement for a late Elizabethan gardener.

Four hundred years later and still in print, Gerard's *Herball* is treasured for its scientific and historical interest, all of it couched in matchless Elizabethan English.

The Re-invention of the Cottage Garden

It was during this relatively prosperous period that the country gentry began to notice what a seemingly uncomplicated, pastoral lifestyle the cottagers lived. This coincided with the eighteenth-century idea of an "estate park" falling from favor. Much of the destruction of the old villages and their cottages had occurred when landowners embraced the "agricultural park" style of landscaping, which emphasized long, uninterrupted vistas with man-made lakes, large trees and extensive lawns. More often than not, there was a cluster of laborers' cottages in the way, so they were leveled to provide an uncluttered panorama for the squire and his family. A knave known as "Capability" Brown (1716–83) was largely responsible for this fashion, aided and abetted by another rogue, Humphrey Repton (1725–1818), but by mid-Victorian times, these parks (which were the Georgian equivalent to modern golf courses — stark and sterile) were considered passé, and two new styles emerged to take their place.

The first was the practice of "carpet bedding," which is mercifully rare these days. Thousands of dwarf annuals were planted in elaborate designs that, from a distance, did indeed look like intricate Oriental carpets. The expense and labor required to pull these designs off made it impossible for most private homes to continue the practice (garish at best) after World War I. No garden worthy of the name should have to be viewed from a distance in order for it to make visual sense.

It was the second style, however, that made the biggest impression on many members of the aristocracy, and this was the cottage garden style. Already much of Britain had become highly industrialized, and then as now, people living in urban centers longed for a simpler way of life. The cottage garden already existed, it already had a distinguished history, and it was just waiting to make a comeback.

Foremost among the new proponents of the cottage garden style (albeit an amended, more floriferous version) was William Robinson (1838–1935). His inspiring book *The English Flower Garden* was first published in 1883 and is still in print. In it he rails against carpet bedding, topiary and formal design with refreshing abandon, stating out loud what so many of us say only under our breath. Instead of lengthy epistles on design, he emphasized the merits of each individual plant and lovingly described most of the flowers that we still think of as being essential to any English cottage garden, in whatever country it exists.

Robinson gardened for most of his life on 200 acres in Sussex at a house called Gravetye Manor. Many plants still in commerce bear this name, the result of Robinson's careful selections over the course of 50 years of dedicated observation. Early each summer as Robinson's summer snowflake (*Leucojum aestivum* 'Gravetye Giant') blooms in my garden, I pause to thank him for his sparkling, fragrant legacy. Most importantly, he legitimized the concept of informal planting, mimicking nature rather than glorifying mankind's ability to control and manipulate the environment.

His attractive theory proved to be highly persuasive for Victorian gentry already fed up with foul-smelling town life. In consequence, nothing short of a building-boom occurred as lords and ladies built elaborate "cottages" complete with servants'

This etching (c. 1885) by my great-grandfather, Charles Dobson (1862–1934) bucked the prevailing Victorian trend that seemed to endlessly romanticize cottage life. The trees are bare, so it is presumably either late autumn or early spring, and certainly cold, but only a wisp of smoke leaves the chimney. There is a duck pond and beehives, but where is the garden? Judging by the state of the thatched roof, these cottagers likely depended on the local landlord for both food and lodging.

quarters — a notion that would have seemed ludicrous only a century before.

Nevertheless, this migration to the country resulted in the construction of some charming cottages and gardens, many of which, sadly, no longer exist. Luckily for us, watercolorist Helen Allingham RWS, (1848–1926) was ready, brush in hand, to record these mid to late Victorian interpretations of what a cottage garden could potentially look like, and she did so with great skill and refinement. She is responsible more than anyone else for our modern notion of the ideal cottage garden, and it is this one generation's interpretation that we all subconsciously strive to emulate.

Allingham was married to the Irish poet William Allingham, and both were part of a high-profile literary circle that included Robert Browning, Thomas Carlyle, John Ruskin and Alfred Lord Tennyson. These associations naturally led to some fairly public mutual back-slapping, not to mention several collaborations, such as *The Homes of Tennyson* (1905) illustrated by Helen (and written by Tennyson), all of which contributed to ensuring the continued popularity of the "revised" cottage garden style.

Allingham also painted several pictures at Munstead Wood, the home of that other great gardener, Gertrude Jekyll (1843–1932). Jekyll was a disciple of Robinson's and with him encouraged people to study cottage gardens closely, in order to learn how to transfer the casual lilt of the cottage garden into their own borders.

What many people don't realize about Gertrude Jekyll is that she started out as a painter, but had to abandon art early on due to her quickly deteriorating eyesight. This disability speaks volumes when we consider the Jekyll style — large, informal drifts of plants, their colors splashed about the garden as if they had gone directly from palette to canvas. Of course, the reason for large drifts was that it was the only way she could discern the plants themselves, being incapable of seeing detail from a distance.

So did Jekyll create artists' gardens or cottage gardens? To be fair, I think she created an interesting hybrid of the two. On the one hand, she used color as an artist would, but not in the way you'd find it in a genuine cottage garden — nature doesn't usually reproduce itself in color-coordinated drifts. On the other hand, she encouraged genetic diversity and an informal style, both of which unquestionably had their roots fixed firmly in the cottage garden tradition, and both of which were contrary to the prevailing fashion.

Jekyll wrote many gardening books, some of which are still available and certainly worth reading, providing you can wade through her stodgy prose. In recent years, her influence on cottage gardens has been called into question, since without exception, her projects were on a scale that would dwarf even the largest cottage garden.

Vita Sackville-West (1892–1962), of Bloomsbury group fame and widely considered heiress to the Robinson-Jekyll style, is criticized for much the same reason — informal plantings on relatively massive scales, beginning with her first home at Knole in Kent, and culminating at the renowned Sissinghurst Castle in Kent. Is her celebrated white border reminiscent of an artist's garden or the cottage garden? Again, it's a case of splitting hairs, since the answer undoubtedly is that it's an artist's garden in the cottage garden style.

The great thing about all these somewhat academic debates is that they have the result of leaving twenty-first century North American gardeners a tremendous amount of scope when it comes to planning our own New World cottage gardens. We can't go wrong if we re-adopt the Elizabethan cottage gardeners' pioneer spirit of discovery and critical study when we consider what to plant in our modern cottage gardens. Any self-respecting seventeenth-century gardener would tell you to grow a plant for several seasons before measuring its merits. In addition to a plant's usefulness for cooking or as a herbal remedy, appearance began to be a criterion for the plants located closest to the house. Most importantly, they shouldn't be too invasive, nor should they require too much care. Cottage gardeners were still far too busy keeping body and soul together to be wasting valuable time on horticultural invalids.

It is heartening to remember that cottage garden plants are a pretty tough bunch to begin with. Early cottagers worked long hours and didn't have time to fuss with floral dilettantes. They needed low-maintenance plants, so most traditional cottage garden varieties are robust enough to have survived the vagaries of the last two or three centuries without much human intervention. This should be ample proof of their strong constitutions and their steadfast resistance to flood, drought, plague and pestilence. Their lust for life can be sharply contrasted with so many of the new introductions that seem to disappear after a season or two, having produced only a few sad apologies for flowers on anemic plants.

Not only are most old-fashioned (or heirloom) varieties more vigorous than their modern counterparts, they also smell an awful lot better. Roses are a good case in point. Almost without exception all old roses have a scent so wonderful that it's paradoxically ethereal and sinful all at once. Not so the newer hybrid teas. They have been bred for continuous bloom, a statuesque form, and thick long-lasting petals in some rather loud colors not found in nature. As most of them are also completely scentless, what's the point? Surely half the fun of roses is their fragrance.

By growing heirloom varieties, we further help to increase the genetic diversity not only of our own gardens and communities, but of the world. Many of the old varieties have been lost, but it's amazing how many have survived in quiet, out-of-the-way places, just waiting to be re-discovered and re-embraced. I like to imagine that if I were sent back two centuries in a time machine, I could at least seek out some local gardeners and be able to communicate reasonably intelligently about the contents of their gardens.

And if those gardeners could be transported to the future, to our gardens, I like to think they would recognize the great gardening tradition they have bequeathed to us, for the cottage garden style and the latitude it affords us is as useful and relevant today as it was for gardeners 300 years ago.

∽ Victorians Whose Art Most Effectively Defined the Cottage Garden Style

Helen Allingham (1848–1926) The best known and most accomplished of the cottage garden artists, she specialized in watercolors.

Edward Kington Brice (1860–1948) Primarily a painter of landscapes; the paintings of the few cottage gardens he did record are exceptionally well executed.

Ernest Albert Chadwick (1876–?) Also better known for his landscapes, he too painted a number of delightful cottage garden scenes.

Birket Foster (1825–1899) Helen Allingham's neighbor in Surrey and an accomplished artist in his own right, he was something of a mentor to her, greatly influencing her work.

CHAPTER THREE ∽

Creating the Cottage Garden

THE FIRST DISAPPOINTMENT THAT many North American gardeners encounter when attempting to reproduce the cottage garden style is that so much of the traditional plant material isn't reliably hardy across most of North America. It's true that the Pacific Northwest and British Columbia enjoy a climate similar to Britain's, but in most other parts of the continent, our extremes of weather inflict a limiting factor. Perhaps it's too cold in the winter, or too hot in the summer, too windy in the spring, or too dry all year round. Maybe it's all four. Whatever the situation, however, a cottage garden is definitely within your reach—you just have to use plant material that is appropriate to your area if you're to be successful. And that's what most of this book is about: how to adapt the English cottage garden style to your conditions.

As a quick reference guide to each plant, refer to the plant portrait box accompanying each entry. You'll be able to determine at a glance whether a plant prefers sun or shade, when it blooms and what it looks good with, how tall it will get, and what sort of soil it requires.

When trying to sort out which plants will thrive in your area, common sense dictates that the easiest thing to do will be to observe what the neighbors grow, and how various plants perform for them. Strike up a conversation if you're feeling gregarious—locals can be a veritable fount of information and are usually happy to throw in a little unsolicited advice as a bonus.

Originally intended to keep the livestock in and the wildlife out, fences today primarily delineate property boundaries. Nevertheless, their importance to the cottage garden style cannot be ignored and is perfectly demonstrated in this portrait: precious roses and delphinium within the enclosure, coupled with more expendable poppies on the outside periphery.

CLIMATIC ZONES

You'll probably want to know what your zone is, since this data is included in most catalogs and on plant tags. Canada and the United States have slightly different scales for determining climatic zones, but it's the easiest thing in the world to translate. If you're looking at a plant listed as hardy to USDA zone 5 but you live in Canada, just add 1, and you'll know that it's hardy to zone 6 as defined by Agriculture Canada. Similarly, a plant listed in Canada as hardy to zone 4, would only be hardy to USDA zone 3 (subtract 1).

Knowing what your zone is will provide you with a rough guide to the perimeters within which you can expect to work. Of course, every experienced gardener will regale you with stories about how he or she has pushed the limit and grown plants previously thought too tender for the region. Often what these people are describing is a microclimate peculiar to their particular garden. We all have them to some degree: possibly a sunny south-facing wall where the spring bulbs always seem to pop up long before they do anywhere else, or a sheltered low-lying area where water tends to collect. Working with your microclimates by planting species that enjoy these unique conditions will allow you to increase the variety of plants you're able to cultivate, while at the same time providing them with optimum growing conditions.

The various climatic zones are largely based on an area's coldest average temperature, since all plants have a minimum temperature range below which they can't survive. What the zone system doesn't take into account, however, is that all plants also have a maximum temperature above which they can't survive, and this is especially relevant in North America, where our summers may be briefer, but are usually hotter and drier, than their British equivalent. It is these conditions that cause clever gardeners to use indigenous plant species and their cultivars, since such plants are already adapted to the local environment. This difference in summer heat also explains why the British have such a difficult time growing good tomatoes and corn — they're simply unable to supply the requisite heat.

WIND

In addition to extremes of heat, another influence often overlooked is the effect of wind on plants. Most of us know that in the summer wind sucks all the moisture from plant tissues as well as from the soil surface, but it does the same in winter as well. Wind is especially hard on evergreens as they continue to respire (although at a reduced rate) throughout the winter months. Cold winds can result in tip injury and dieback, and eventually death. Many rosemary and lavender plants are alive today because they were over-wintered in a cold frame or unheated porch, and so were protected from windy conditions. It isn't the temperature that makes them give up the ghost, it's the desiccation!

In the colder parts of North America, and on the High Plains specifically, another winter phenomenon also comes into play, that of the dreaded "frost/thaw" cycle. In the East it's known as the "January Thaw," and in the West, the warm winds that raise the winter temperature many degrees in the course of a few hours are called "chinooks." Whatever the name, the effect is the same. Warmer temperatures melt the protective covering of snow and warm the soil sufficiently to thaw the top couple of inches or centimeters. Inevitably the mercury soon plummets, and the ground freezes again. This cycle can occur many times in the space of a day or two, and as the soil expands and contracts, it heaves plant roots up onto the soil surface. Shallowly rooted plants are especially vulnerable. The only way to protect against this lethal cycle is to apply mulch in the early winter once the ground is already frozen.

Many gardeners think that a layer of mulch helps to keep the soil from freezing, but in fact the opposite is true. Winter mulch is applied to keep the ground frozen, and to avoid letting it thaw out. Aside from heaving up root systems, a premature thaw can also break a plant's winter dormancy months too early. This is especially crucial for roses that may be only borderline hardy: Apply mulch or hill up soil after the ground is frozen, and don't remove it until you're certain that spring is well under way.

ALTITUDE

Altitude also has an effect on plant material as anyone who has ever tried to grow alpines at sea level will tell you. On average, the temperature drops one degree Fahrenheit for every 250 feet in elevation . In addition, lofty peaks result in higher light intensities, making it necessary to grow some plants that normally require only part shade in full shade, while many sun-loving plants will be quite content with partly shaded conditions.

In many North American cottage gardens (especially those in rural areas that depend on well water), turning on the hose is not an option. With the additional stress of exposed windy slopes, it's important to choose plant material that can cope with these conditions. Nonetheless, this restriction seems a small price to pay for a panorama like this one.

RAINFALL

Another point to consider when selecting plant material is the amount of rainfall your region receives. For most North Americans it isn't enough, and we often end up relying on sprinklers, drip hoses and underground irrigation systems. In really dry areas, however, restrictions are placed on watering gardens, and water shortages are a serious fact of life. If this is the case where you live, it will be important for you to choose drought-tolerant plants, many of which will undoubtedly be native to your region.

SOIL

Before you start deciding which plants to include in your cottage garden, you'll need to know what type of soil you have. What's its pH? Is it acid or alkaline, and how about the texture — is it clay or sand? Different plants have different preferences for both soil pH and texture.

In general, the optimum soil pH for the largest number of plants is slightly acidic to neutral — 6.5 to 7.0 on the pH scale. If the soil becomes too acidic, you'll find yourself restricted to blueberries (*Vaccinium* spp.) and rhododendrons, and your plants may have trouble extracting enough nitrogen from the soil for normal growth. If it's too alkaline, you'll have to content yourself with baby's breath (*Gypsophila paniculata*) and asparagus, and you may find that some plants show signs of phosphorus and iron deficiency. Inexpensive test kits for measuring soil pH are available at most garden centers, or if you want more extensive testing done, (including nutrient values), you should contact your state Department of Agriculture in the United States, or your provincial Ministry of Agriculture in Canada. Universities with a department of soil science and most agricultural colleges also perform soil tests.

Amending your soil with liming materials to increase its alkalinity is quite easy and inexpensive. Dolomitic lime (high in calcium and magnesium) can be dug into the soil at a rate of about 6 lb. per 100 sq. ft. (2.7 kilograms per 9 square meters), as can aragonite and calcitic lime (both high in calcium) at about the same rate. Wood ashes can also be added in small quantities (2 lb. per 100 sq. ft./900 grams per 9 square meters), but don't overdo it or you'll end up with soil that's too high in potassium.

Amending soil to increase its acidity is a little more difficult. Some gardeners simply excavate the existing soil to a depth of about 18 inches (45 centimeters) and replace it with peat moss and loam in equal amounts — I'd also recommend adding some extra compost. Alternatively, elemental sulfur at a

---

∾ Drought-tolerant Perennial Plants

Dry conditions needn't frustrate your dream of creating a beautiful cottage garden. Any of the following plants (many of them native) will thrive in dry areas while providing a succession of bloom throughout the summer.

* Black-eyed Susan — *Rudbeckia fulgida* 'Goldsturm' — Zones 4–9
* Blanket flower — *Gaillardia x grandiflora* — Zones 4–8
* Butterfly weed — *Asclepias tuberosa* — Zones 4–9
Cupid's dart — *Catanache caerulea* — Zones 5–8
* Gayfeather — *Liatris spicata* — Zones 4–9
Globe thistle — *Echinops ritro* — Zones 4–9
Golden Marguerite — *Anthemis tinctoria* — Zones 4–8
Lavender — *Lavandula angustifolia* — Zones 5–9
Maltese cross — *Lychnis chalcedonica* — Zones 4–8
* Purple coneflower — *Echinacea purpurea* — Zones 4–9
Sea holly — *Eryngium alpinum* — Zones 4–8
Sea thrift — *Armeria maritima* — Zones 4–7
Stonecrop — *Sedum spectabile* — Zones 4–9
Sweet sultan — *Centaurea macrocephala* — Zones 3–8
Yarrow — *Achillea millefolium* — Zones 3–8

* = native

---

rate of 2 lb. per 100 sq. ft. (900 grams per 9 square meters), or gypsum (calcium sulfate) at a rate of 5 lb. per 100 sq. ft. (2 kilograms per 9 square meters) will be an effective means of acidifying your soil. If you choose this method you'll notice that pH rates begin to climb again after a year or two, and another application to re-acidify your soil may be necessary. Composted pine needles or a shredded oak leaf mulch also help to acidify soil gradually. If you're in a position to hand-water the area, add a tablespoon or two (15 or 30 milliliters) of white vinegar to your watering can — the acetic acid (5 percent) it contains will further help to neutralize alkalinity without damaging plant roots.

Once you know what your pH range is, you need to know about your soil's texture. The opposite ends of the soil spectrum, both of which you'll want to avoid, are very light sandy soil and heavy clay. As with pH levels, the best place to be is somewhere in the middle range, with a soil that contains both sand (good for drainage) and clay (high in nutrients), with lots of organic matter. This type of soil is called loam.

Whether you start out with sand or clay, if you

❧ Soil Amendments

Depending on where you live in North America, certain soil amendments will be more widely available in your area than others. Unless you're a good gardener below the soil surface, you can't expect to be a good gardener above it. Any of the following 15 soil amendments will go a long way toward ensuring your success.

Amendment	Primary Impact	Notes
Alfalfa meal	High in organic matter	Contains a natural growth hormone (triaconatol)
Bloodmeal	High in nitrogen	10–0–0
Bone meal	High in phosphorus	1–11–0, and a good source of calcium
Coffee grounds	Source of nitrogen	Helps to acidify soil, best added to the compost heap
Compost (homemade)	Balanced N-P-K	High in organic matter
Compost (mushroom)	High in organic matter	Caution: May contain pesticide residue
Eggshells	High in calcium	Contains micronutrients
Epsom salts	Source of magnesium & sulfur	Soil balancer
Fish meal	High in nitrogen	5–3–3
Grass clippings	Organic matter	0.5–0.2–0.5
Kelp meal	High in potassium	1.5–0.5–2.5, also contains micronutrients
Oak leaves	Organic matter	Good source of phosphorus
Peat moss	Organic matter	pH between 3.0–4.5, good for acid-loving plants
Wood ashes	High in potassium	Apply sparingly unless well-leached
Worm castings	Organic matter	Good source of nutrients and micronutrients

*Cool-season annual crops like lettuce (*Lactuca sativus*) and dill (*Anethum graveolens*) can be seeded in early spring to be harvested by early summer, making available additional growing space for warm-season transplants such as lima beans, okra and hot peppers.*

want to end up with loam, you must get to work straight away and start adding organic matter to the soil. It's the best way to improve your existing soil, and while it may take a few seasons to get it right, it's the most permanent long-term solution for correcting less than perfect soil. Dig up the soil as much as possible, and when it's loose and permeable, dig in the organic matter. Compost, composted manure, shredded leaves and seaweed all make first-class amendments. Soil nutrients can be given an extra boost at the same time with the addition of a little bloodmeal and bone meal mixed into the soil solution.

Despite these amendments, you may still find yourself with soil that's sandy and acidic or clayey and alkaline for the first few years. Don't panic, though — there are lots of plants that prefer these more borderline conditions, and since we've already established that we have a much greater base of plant material to choose from than early cottage gardeners did, this obstacle should not prove insurmountable.

In any discussion of soil, we can't ignore the issue of nutrients. While the addition of chemical fertilizers may give plants a nutrient "shot in the arm," a far wiser long-term approach is to improve the overall quality and texture of your soil, while at the same time providing nutrients that remain fixed within the soil profile. This objective is easily achieved with the addition of soil amendments and organic fertilizers. Chemical fertilizers tend to be leached out of the upper layers of the soil with the first heavy rainfall, while organic amendments stabilize the soil and remain available to plants for a much longer period of time.

The immediate nutrient availability of soil fertilizers and conditioners always appears as three numbers separated by hyphens (e.g., soluble chemical fertilizers for flowering plants are generally within the 15–30–15 range). These numbers represent the percent of available nitrogen (N), phosphorus (P) and potassium (K), always in that order. Chemical fertilizers tend to have high numbers, while organic fertilizers and composted manures tend to have very low numbers (composted cow manure is typically about 0.6–0.2–0.5, for example). Don't be put off by this: all that it indicates is that the nutrients are available in smaller quantities over a much greater length of time. Plants naturally prefer this approach as opposed to an overdose of chemical adrenaline.

All plants require nitrogen (N) as it is responsible for green leafy growth, which is why we traditionally add such high amounts of it to turfgrass. However, flowering plants require much lower levels, and over-fertilization with nitrogen will induce plants to produce lush foliage, with nary a bloom.

Phosphorus (P) is important to the establishment of good root growth, which is why transplant solutions tend to be swimming in it. It also induces flowering in most plants as it is a vital component in the development of plants' reproductive organs.

Potassium (K) is important for the overall smooth functioning of many plant processes and is especially important in the formation of seeds.

In addition to these three major nutrients, there are many more (called micronutrients) such as iron, zinc, copper and manganese which are also vital to healthy plant growth. Homemade compost is rich in micronutrients as are most organic fertilizers.

CROP ROTATION

The successional planting referred to in Chapter 1 – planting radishes among the dying foliage of bulbs, for example – also ensures an opportunity to keep your soil rich and healthy. Every time a crop is harvested, or a plant is moved, compost or composted manure should be added to the soil to keep it "fat," as the Elizabethan gardeners would have said. It makes sense to think of the soil as fat or thin, and in turn to think of "feeding" the soil, rather than merely fertilizing it. Really fat soil will gradually provide nutrients to plants as needed

◊ Heavy- and Light-Feeding Vegetables

Heavy	Light
Asparagus	Carrots
Beets	Swiss Chard
Broccoli	Garlic
Brussels sprouts	Leeks
Cabbage	Onions
Cardoon	Parsnips
Cauliflower	Potatoes
Celery	Rutabagas
Corn	Salsify
Cucumbers	Scorzonera
Eggplant	Shallots
Lettuce	Turnips
Okra	
Spinach	
Tomatoes	

for years and years. Anorexic soil will only lead to tears.

Modern farmers are also once again espousing the idea of growing different plants on the same soil, but in their case, they'd call it "crop rotation." The idea is the same — getting two different crops a year out of the same patch of land, or at the very least, not growing the same crop on the same land for two years in a row. The advantage of harvesting more than one crop per season is obvious, but there are also less apparent benefits to be gained.

Some crops, such as corn, cabbage and tomatoes, are heavy feeders, quickly depleting the soil of many available nutrients. By following heavy feeders with light feeders (such as carrots, rutabagas or onions), there's no need to amend the soil with additional nutrient sources between crops, saving time, energy and money. Although there are a

∾ Plants for Acidic or Alkaline Soil

Early cottage gardeners didn't have a lot of time to coddle their plants so they turned to ones that would perform well in their conditions. These will give you the cottage garden feel if you're gardening in especially acid or alkaline conditions. You will notice that native North American plants tend to like acid soil and many plants tolerant of alkaline soil are Eurasian.

COTTAGE GARDEN PLANTS SUITABLE FOR ACIDIC SOIL
* Alumroot — *Heuchera* cultivars — Zones 4–8, Perennial
* Bayberry — *Myrica pensylvanica* — Zones 3–6, Shrub
* Black cohosh — *Cimicifuga racemosa* — Zones 3–8, Perennial
* Blueberry — *Vaccinium* spp. — Zones 3–8, Shrub
* Fringed bleeding heart — *Dicentra eximia* — Zones 4–8, Perennial
* Lady's slipper orchid — *Cypripedium* spp. — Zones 5–8, Perennial
* Mountain laurel — *Kalmia latifolia* — Zones 5–9, Shrub
* Potato — *Solanum tuberosum* — Annual vegetable
* Rhododendron — 'Catawbiense' hybrids — Zones 5–8, Shrub, small tree
* Serviceberry — *Amelanchier canadensis* — Zones 4–8, Shrub
* Turtlehead — *Chelone obliqua* — Zones 4–9, Perennial
* Wintergreen — *Gaultheria procumbens* — Zones 3–8, Evergreen sub-shrub

COTTAGE GARDEN PLANTS SUITABLE FOR ALKALINE SOIL
Apple — *Malus* cultivars — Hardiness variable, Fruit tree
Baby's breath — *Gypsophila paniculata* — Zones 4–9, Perennial
Bearded iris — *Iris* spp. and cultivars — Zones 3–9, Perennial
Bear's breeches — *Acanthus spinosus* — Zones 5–9, Perennial
Black mulberry — *Morus nigra* — Zones 5–9, Fruit tree
Chinese wisteria — *Wisteria sinensis* spp. and cultivars — Zones 5–8, Woody climber
French lilac — *Syringa vulgaris* and cultivars — Zones 4–8, Flowering shrub
Globe amaranth — *Gomphrena glabosa* — Annual
Lady Banks rose — *Rosa banksiae* and cultivars — Zones 7–9, Climbing rose
Leopard's bane — *Doronicum* spp. — Zones 4–8, Perennial
Marigold (French and African) — *Tagetes* spp. — Annual
Night-scented stock — *Matthiola longipetala* — Annual
Pot marigold — *Calendula officinalis* and cultivars — Annual
Purple mullein — *Verbascum phoeniceum* — Zones 4–8, Perennial
Regal lily — *Lilium regale* — Zones 4–7, Bulb
* = native

couple of exceptions to the rule, you'll notice that heavy feeders usually produce their crop above ground, while light feeders produce theirs below the soil surface.

In addition, both insect and disease organisms depend on a steady supply of target plants (those plants they require for food and shelter) if they are to thrive. The more target plants, the better, and the longer they're present, the more pests they'll nurture. By shifting crops around from field to field, farmers help to frustrate the designs of these unwanted guests, making it difficult for them to accumulate in large numbers on a particular piece of land, either in the soil or on the plants.

That is why every ministry or department of agriculture across North America advises, for instance, not to plant potatoes, tomatoes, peppers or eggplants in the same soil for two years running. These plants are all members of the Solanaceae or nightshade family and are prone to many similar diseases that can build up in the soil over time. By rotating these fruits and vegetables, we are able to disrupt this detrimental cycle. Starving unwanted organisms by employing crop rotation is as important as feeding your soil with compost and rotted manure to keep the beneficial insects and organisms healthy and fat. The cottage garden satisfies both these objectives quite unselfconsciously, due simply to its design (or lack thereof).

PESTS AND DISEASES

Today, we face far more choices than the traditional cottage gardeners did, and one of the most important ones concerns methods of dealing with diseases and insects. Whether you decide to garden with or

Beneficial insects provide a frontline defense against unwanted insect pests, but cottage gardeners must plant species that will provide the beneficials with the habitat and food they need in order to stay strong and healthy. In addition to all members of the Umbelliferae or parsley family (see list on p. 36), I wouldn't be without perennial baby's breath (Gypsophila repens) and blue alkanet (Anchusa officinalis). How many ladybugs can you count?

without chemical pesticides is a matter between you and your conscience. Certainly, if you're planning to use pesticides on edibles, you should be very careful indeed. The fact of the matter is that you shouldn't need to apply pesticides at all, because cottage gardens rarely have any serious insect or disease problems. What with the flowers all mixed up haphazardly in a colorful riot, and fruit and vegetables planted in small patches throughout the garden, it's hard for a pest to find a welcoming spot in which to thrive. It's easier to fly next door where all the cabbages are planted in neat rows, waiting to be transformed into cabbage moth hatcheries.

What the cottage garden avoids creating (again, by its lack of design) is a monoculture — the practice of planting large areas with one species. Insects and disease build up quickly in a monoculture, unlike the cottage garden where the plants' genetic diversity ensures that no one pest gets much of a foothold.

In addition to the plethora of homemade remedies that organic gardeners employ to combat pests, there are two that are widely available and quite safe to use on edibles and around children and pets. One is insecticidal soap, which controls a wide variety of garden insects, and the other is Bordeaux mixture, which is a copper sulfate solution that is effective against a wide spectrum of plant diseases. Dormant oil and sulfur sprays are also effective in controlling many insect and disease pests on woody plant material and are applied at the end of winter.

Don't be too hard on yourself if you feel that your back is to the wall, and you want to bring out the heavy arsenal. I have been known to resort to a commercial chemical rose spray myself when I thought that I was in danger of losing a particularly rare old Bourbon rose.

The trouble with chemical sprays is that they're non-selective and kill absolutely everything they hit. If you monitor your plants for problems on a regular basis, you'll be much more likely to be aware of potential trouble early on, and any affliction caught early is easier to treat. Chemical sprays are, after all, like using a sledgehammer instead of a fly swatter.

One of the best fly swatter approaches is to get nature on your side in a big way and import some beneficial bugs. These are now widely available both at garden centers and by mail order. Importing a crew of ladybugs (*Hippodamia convergens*) at the first sign of aphids is an excellent way to deal with the problem all season long. Gardeners often complain that the bugs fly away, and of course, some do, but

❧ Members of the Parsley (Umbelliferae) Family that Attract Beneficial Insects

Angelica — *Angelica archangelica* — Zones 3–9, Biennial herb

Carrot — *Daucus carota* var. *sativus* — Annual vegetable

Celery — *Apium graveolens* var. *dulce* — Annual vegetable

Chervil — *Anthriscus cerefolium* — Annual herb

Coriander/Cilantro — *Coriandrum sativum* — Annual herb

Cow parsley — *Anthriscus sylvestris* — Zones 6–9, Biennial (look for the cultivar 'Ravenswing')

Cow parsnip — *Heracleum mantegazzianum* — Zones 2–8, Biennial

Fennel — *Foeniculum vulgare* — Zones 4–8, Short-lived perennial herb (look for bronze and purple cultivars)

Golden chervil — *Chaerophyllum aureum* — Zones 5–8, Perennial

Goutweed — *Aegopodium podagraria* 'Variegatum' — Zones 3–9, Perennial groundcover

Lovage — *Levisticum officinale* — Zones 2–8, Perennial herb

Masterwort — *Astrantia major* and cultivars — Zones 4–8, Perennial

Parsley — *Petroselinum crispum* — Zones 4–7, Biennial herb

Sea holly — *Eryngium* spp. — Zones 4–8, Perennial

Sweet Cicely — *Myrrhis odorata* — Zones 3–8, Self-seeding perennial enough stay in the garden to keep the predator-to-pest ratio within acceptable bounds.

Before importing ladybugs or any other beneficial insect to your garden, you should do a little homework on the life cycle of each species you are considering using. Most gardeners don't realize that it's the larval stage of the ladybug that is the most voracious feeder, but because it looks like a small black alligator we often don't equate it with anything even remotely ladybug-like. Worse still, we may think it's another pest to combat, decide we're defeated, and reach for the spray equipment. Remember that beneficial insects take some time to settle down. First they'll look for water, so it's a good idea to spray plants in the target areas with water before you release them. Next they'll look for food — Aphid Surprise — and if your garden is to their liking, they'll then set about raising a family.

Another great aphid predator is the gall (or aphid) midge (*Aphidoletes aphidimyza*), whose larvae first paralyze and then suck the juices out of aphids at night. If you're looking for entertainment as well as pest control, these shy creatures are probably not for you. Green lacewings (*Chrysopa carnea*) are another favorite and control lots of garden pests, including mealybugs, spider mites and whitefly larvae. As with the ladybug, it is the larvae that do the most good, and they too look like diminutive alligators.

Whatever you do, remember that all beneficial insects are very susceptible to sprays, even organic ones, so you must make a decision early on in the season as to which it will be: sprays or beneficials. Many beneficials will be attracted to your garden simply by virtue of what you have planted there. One of the best plant families to invite into your cottage garden if you want to attract the good guys are the *Umbelliferas* or members of the parsley family. Queen Anne's lace or wild carrot (*Daucus carota*) is a good example of what a typical flower in this genus looks like. Members of this family all have hundreds of minute white or pale green flowers arranged on umbels (think "umbrellas") whose nectar is very attractive to many beneficials. Try planting some masterwort and sea holly, or let some lovage and bronze fennel plants flower and go to seed. You'll be amazed to discover the number of fascinating creatures for which these plants provide an ideal habitat.

GRASS

In this era of front lawns being torn up and turned into prairie meadows or native woodlands, it's much easier to convince people to say *ciao* to the turf than it used to be. Not so long ago, a lawn-less yard was a sure sign that the residents had descended into irrevocable moral turpitude. That's not the case now. In many parts of the continent, the infestation of lawn grubs has also reached epidemic proportions, making the goal of a perfect green carpet more difficult, time-consuming and expensive than ever to achieve. Moreover, people have an increasing aversion to the pesticides and high nitrogen fertilizers so commonly and cavalierly applied to turfgrass, and so culpable where groundwater contamination is concerned.

Picture yourself trying to explain to a Georgian cottage gardener why you tie up so much valuable real estate in the pursuit of the perfect lawn. I'm certain you'd be met with a look of sheer amazement. Nevertheless, you may opt to remove your grass in stages rather than all at once — and there's certainly nothing wrong with this approach, providing you possess patience (which it behooves every

Vancouver garden consultant Therese D'Monte illustrates how turfgrass can best be used in a cottage garden setting.

The "thin green line" effectively links together all sections of the garden, while at the same time providing a visual contrast,

offsetting the plants within the borders. Needless to say, the immaculate edging didn't happen by itself!

gardener to cultivate). One use for grass in a cottage garden that doesn't look out of place, is to employ it as a pathway surface. Granted it will tend to creep into your borders, but if you don't mind a little extra weeding, you needn't be absolutely turf-less.

There are a myriad of ways to dispose of turf, but once it's off by whatever means you choose, what do you do with it? One option is to turn it over (grass side down) and bury it about 1 foot (30 centimeters) deep. Cover the area with 1 foot (30 centimeters) of topsoil. The nitrogen-rich turf will die and slowly decompose, adding an extra layer of organic matter to the soil. The best time to do this is in the fall to ensure good decomposition, though it's also possible to do it in the spring. Another alternative is to create a berm with the leftover sod. Decide what part of the garden could benefit from a little man-made elevation and then arrange the turf in a heap (grass side down again). The turf will form a solid base for the berm, which should then be covered all over with an additional foot (30 centimeters) of topsoil or triple-mix. Rocks may be put in place before the topsoil is added to provide additional plant pockets and stability.

Once the berm is completed and ready to plant, resist the urge to plant short specimens around the bottom, and crown it with tall plants. I made this mistake in my salad days, the forlorn result culminating in a large berm with two holly bushes awkwardly perched on the summit. Fortunately for me, they promptly died, and mercifully no record of their fleeting existence survives. In nature, tall plants grow at the bottom of berms and hillocks, with short plants on top. My advice then, is to be natural.

TREES

The only trees that can be said to be truly authentic to the cottage garden style are fruit and nut trees. The notion of planting a tree for shade alone or for winter interest would have been totally foreign to

---

∾ Native Trees for the Cottage Garden

In spite of trees not being authentic to the English cottage garden style, many North Americans will feel the need for larger trees to provide shade and (especially in urban areas) privacy. The following 15 native trees will all fit in with the cottage garden style admirably.

American mountain ash (*Sorbus americana*)
American smoke tree (*Cotinus obovatus*)
Basswood (*Tilia americana*)
Black gum (*Nyssa sylvatica*)
Flowering dogwood (*Cornus florida*)

Kentucky coffee tree (*Gymnocladus dioicus*)
Northern red oak (*Quercus rubra*)
Pagoda dogwood (*Cornus alternifolia*)
River birch (*Betula nigra* 'Heritage')
Redbud (*Cercis canadensis*)
Red maple (*Acer rubrum*)
Serviceberry (*Amelanchier laevis*)
Tulip tree (*Liriodendron tulipifera*)
White ash (*Fraxinus americana*)
White pine (*Pinus strobus*)

cottage gardeners. A tree was worthy of space in the garden only for what it could produce for the table. Most of these traditional trees weren't large and were further pruned back to reduce their height for ease of harvest.

This approach is fine if you're starting from scratch and have a virtually blank canvas with which to begin, but most homeowners inherit trees when they purchase their properties. If you find yourself with some large specimens, don't despair — they'll add height to your garden, and at the same time furnish habitat for wildlife. Often they'll be shrewdly utilized as living supports for vines like clematis or ivy. In addition, tree removal is often impractical and expensive, not to mention contrary to municipal by-laws in many areas.

Most traditional cottage garden plants require full sun, but there are many alternative species, a lot of them native, that will provide the same effect as the sun-lovers, but are quite happy growing in shady conditions. Planting under trees presents a different problem however. Not only is there shade to contend with, but there's usually dry, nutrient-poor soil to deal with as well. Clearly, in any battle for moisture and nourishment between a tree and a plant, the tree will win every time. Conveniently for us, there are many plants that will tolerate, even thrive in, these difficult conditions.

In addition to the usual groundcovers, certain ferns will prosper in dry shade, although they may require extra water until they become established. English ivy (*Hedera helix*), a cottage garden plant from way back, will grow almost anywhere once it settles down and is available in some very attractive cultivars. Really tough spots may call for some variegated goutweed (*Aegopodium podagraria* 'Variegatum'), but

---

❧ More Plants for Dry Shade

Gardeners who are in the process of converting their lawn and borders to a classic cottage garden are likely to be faced with the problem of well-established trees that cast shade and extract a great deal of water and nourishment from the soil. The following plants will tolerate these harsh conditions.

Blue holly — *Ilex x meserveae* — Zones 4–9, Evergreen shrub, requires both male and female varieties for berry production. 'Blue Princess' and 'Blue Prince' are especially hardy.
❧ Canada columbine — *Aquilegia canadensis* — Zones 3–8, Self-seeding perennial
Deadnettle — *Lamium maculatum* and cultivars — Zones 4–8, Perennial flowering groundcover
❧ Fringe cups — *Tellima grandiflora* and cultivars — Zones 4–8, Perennial

Garden comfrey — *Symphytum ibericum* — Zones 5–9, Perennial herb
❧ Labrador violet — *Viola labradorica* — Zones 2–8, Semi-evergreen perennial
Lady's mantle — *Alchemilla mollis* — Zones 4–7, Perennial
❧ Oregon grapeholly — *Mahonia aquifolium* — Zones 6–9, Evergreen shrub
Periwinkle — *Vinca minor* — Zones 4–9, Evergreen sub-shrub

Ferns
Hart's-tongue fern — *Asplenium scolopendrium* — Zones 4–8
Japanese holly fern — *Cyrtomium falcatum* — Zones 6–10
Rusty-back fern — *Asplenium ceterach* — Zones 5–8
Wall fern — *Polypodium vulgare* — Zones 5–8
❧ = native

this plant can be invasive so keep a close eye on it.

Bulbs such as Star of Bethlehem (*Ornithogalum nutans*) and wood hyacinth (*Hyacinthoides hispanica*, syn. *Scilla campanulata*) will multiply freely under trees, providing seasonal interest. The hardy bigroot geranium (*Geranium macrorrhizum*) is vigorous though not invasive, and several plants will cover an area in just a few seasons. The delicate blooms are a bonus to the handsome aromatic foliage, and established clumps will afford effective weed suppression. These shallow-rooted geraniums can be divided yearly. If the foliage begins to look tatty by mid-summer, mow the plants down to their crowns. Given an extra gulp of water, fresh new foliage will appear within two weeks. Mourning widow (*Geranium phaem*), *G. endressii* and *G. renardii* and their cultivars are three other hardy geraniums that make excellent candidates for groupings under trees.

If you find yourself the proud possessor of some mature trees, "pruning up" may be a big part of your solution. All this entails is the removal of the lowest limbs of the tree, so that it's encouraged to "grow up," thereby increasing the height of the canopy, rather than increasing its spread. In turn, this will increase light levels and air circulation below the tree's drip line, enabling you to grow plants that require some sun at the base of the tree.

One of the best ways to find which plants tolerate dry shade in your own garden is by trial and error. Obviously, the plant should be vigorous and capable of multiplying easily. Any plant with these characteristics will soon make its presence felt, so try transplanting some of the progeny to difficult areas of the garden to see how they perform. Invariably, different plants will prosper in different gardens, and what grows like a weed in one location may languish in another. Don't be afraid to experiment.

Inheriting a property that contains established trees need not be an obstacle to North American cottage gardeners. Pruning off the lower branches (a process know as "limbing up") increases air circulation and light levels to the adjacent garden. Here, the statuesque tree trunks that remain form a stalwart backdrop to a brilliant floral display.

❧ Fruit and Nut Varieties Suitable for Informal Cottage Garden Hedges

The old cottagers always included some small trees and shrubs in their hedge-borders that would furnish extra fruit and nuts to expand the family diet. While today's cottage gardeners are more likely to be interested in attracting birds, butterflies and wildlife to their hedges, the following trees and shrubs will perform to perfection in either role.

Apples — *Malus* spp. Providing that apple varieties are grafted on to a hardy dwarf root stock, almost all apple cultivars are suitable. The following three cultivars are hardy to Zone 1.
'Heyer #20'
'Parkland'
'Rutherford'

Blackberry — *Rubus* spp.
'Chester' — Zone 4
'Darrow' — Zone 5
'Thornless' — Zone 3

Blueberry — *Vaccinium* spp.
'Bluecrop' — Zone 5
'North Country' — Zone 2
'Patriot' — Zone 4

Black Chokeberry — *Aronia melanocarpa*
A. melanocarpa elata — Zone 3
'Viking' — Zone 4

Black Currant (*Ribes* spp.)
'Boskoop Giant' — Zone 2
'Consort' — Zone 3
'Wellington XXX' — Zone 5

Red Currant (*Ribes* spp.)
'Cherry' — Zone 3
'Random' — Zone 5
'Red Lake' — Zone 1

White Currant (*Ribes* spp.)
'White Pearl' — Zone 5

Elderberry (*Sambucus canadensis*)
'John's' — Zone 3

'Victoria' — Zone 3
'York' — Zone 3

American Filbert (Hazelnut) (*Corylus americana* hybrids)
'Bixby' — Zones 5–9
'Buchanan' — Zones 6–9
'Reed' — Zones 6–9

Beaked Filbert (*Corylus cornuta*)
'Gellatly' — Zones 5–9
'Gellatly hybrids' — Zones 4–9

European Filbert (English) (*Corylus avellana*)
'Fusco-rubra' — Zones 5–9
'Pendula' — Zones 5–9
'Rote Zeller' — Zones 5–9

Gooseberry (*Ribes* spp.)
'Captivator' — Zone 4
'Dakota' — Zone 3
'Hinnomaeki' — Zone 3
'Pixwell' — Zone 2

Lingonberry (*Vaccinium vitis-idaea*)
'Red Pearl' — Zone 1
'Regal' — Zone 1
'Splendor' — Zone 1

Japanese Quince (*Chaenomeles* spp.)
'Cooke's Jumbo' — Zone 5
'Quince of Portugal' — Zone 5

Black Raspberries (*Rubus* spp.)
'Bristol' — Zone 5
'Cumberland' — Zone 5
'Himalayan Giant' — Zone 2
'Lowden's Black' — Zone 4

Red Raspberries (*Rubus* spp.)
'Boyne' — Zone 2
'Comet' — Zone 5
'Heritage' — Zone 2
'Latham' — Zone 4

Purple Raspberries (*Rubus* spp.)
'Brandywine' — Zone 4
'Columbian' — Zone 5
'Royalty' — Zone 4

Yellow Raspberries (*Rubus* spp.)
'Fallgold' — Zone 5
'Goldie' — Zone 3
'Honey Queen' — Zone 3

GARDEN STRUCTURES

The majority of the structures in your cottage garden will hardly seem like structures at all, since they are an integral part of most working gardens, whatever the style. The two most important watchwords when considering what to include in your garden must always be "rustic" and "simple." Ornate furnishings strike a discordant note in the cottage garden, and in any case, the cottagers would never have been able to afford them, nor would they have been happy about sacrificing valuable growing space. Elaborate urns, baroque fountains and Greek statuary should be avoided at all costs. Garden structures can certainly act as accents, but they should be subdued enough that they never distract the eye from the real focus of the garden, which is, of course, the plants themselves.

Traditional cottage gardens are usually enclosed by a fence or a shrub border, or both. In North America, a white picket fence will unquestionably be obligatory for purists. Permanent fencing of any kind can prove to be an expensive proposition, especially if you have a large area to cover. In the past, fences and hedges served an important purpose: either to keep the livestock penned within the cottage boundaries, or more frequently, to keep them out. This may not be a concern for twenty-first-century cottage gardeners, but the visual impact that these structures add cannot be ignored.

In North America, many of us opt for a fenceless shrub border in our cottage gardens. Usually these borders are made up of mixed plantings, and ideally they will provide a succession of bloom. While the overall impact is certainly less tidy than a clipped yew hedge, these shrub borders profit the garden with their abundant bloom over an extended period of time, they enhance genetic diversity within the garden, they act as a windbreak, and because they're permanent, they represent a one-time expenditure. This kind of planting will provide a rich (if somewhat disheveled) tapestry.

HEDGE OF ROSES

Another option that adds a truly romantic ambiance to the cottage garden is to plant a hedge of roses. I live across the street from a grade school and I've found that the larger old-fashioned roses I've interplanted with shorter, spiny flowering quince (*Chaenomeles speciosa* 'Texas Scarlet') furnish a splendid garden margin that, in addition to being fragrant, also has the advantage of keeping the little angels off the flower beds. Neighborhood canines also seem increasingly reticent to leave their aqueous calling cards. The main difference between fencing and hedging is that fencing will render the garden impenetrable immediately, while hedging will likely take a few years to fill in and will require some occasional pruning as it matures.

A gate or two providing access between the hedges to the garden beyond is central to the cottage style. In addition to supplying an easily perceptible visual approach, it also helps to establish a permanent entrance or starting point, serving as an incentive to induce visitors to explore farther. These gates are usually of wood, although metal gates seem to work better with stone walls if you're lucky enough to have them. Arches are often mounted above gateways to further frame the garden beyond and to provide support for vines.

❧ Rose Cultivars Suitable for Hedging in Cottage Gardens

Without a doubt, cottage garden pedants will opt for a living hedge in favor of a static fence. The following roses are eminently suited to this purpose, and all are readily available.

Rosa alba cultivars
  'Blanche de Belgique' (white), France 1817, Zone 3
  'Great Maiden's Blush' (light pink), Unknown *c.* 1400,
    Zone 3
  'Konigin von Danemark' (pink), Unknown 1826, Zone 3
Rosa centifolia cultivars
  'Nuit de Young' (Old black moss) (red), France 1845,
    Zone 4
  'Spong' (pink), France 1805, Zone 4
Rosa rugosa cultivars
  'Agnes' (yellow), Canada 1922, Zone 3

'Hansa' (mauve), Holland 1905, Zone 3
'Martin Frobisher' (light pink), Canada 1968, Zone 2
  (first rose in the 'Explorer Series')
'Ruskin' (deep red), USA 1928, Zone 3
'Sir Thomas Lipton' (white), USA 1900, Zone 4
Rosa spinosissima cultivars
  'Harison's Yellow' (Yellow rose of Texas) (yellow),
    USA 1830, Zone 3
  'Hazeldean' (yellow), Canada 1948, Zone 2
  'Stanwell Perpetual' (light pink), England 1838, Zone 3
Agriculture Canada winter-hardy roses
  'Alexander Mackenzie' (deep red), Explorer series —
    Canada 1985, Zone 3
  'John Davis' (pink), Explorer series — Canada 1986, Zone 3
  'Prairie Joy' (pink), Morden series — Canada 1990, Zone 2
  'William Baffin' (medium red), Explorer series — Canada
    1983, Zone 2

Undeniably, some caterpillars are more desirable than others, but to get a color-coordinated combination like this is cause for serious and deliberate celebration. On this caterpillar's menu is Rosa 'Pink Meidiland', introduced by the French firm Meilland in 1985 and hardy to zone 4. Vigorous and disease resistant, this species rose look-alike tolerates harsh roadside conditions.

Arbors and arches can be employed throughout the garden to afford extra opportunities for the cultivation of climbing plants, while at the same time adding height and enticing guests ever farther down the garden path.

Viewed from our vantage point, it often appears that the old cottagers threw many of the design principles that we've been taught to hold dear out the window. After all, design was not a vital consideration, but getting each plant to produce to its full potential was. Nevertheless, they certainly weren't above adding a capricious flounce here and there, providing it didn't tie up valuable garden space.

PATHS

The garden path itself is open to wide interpretation. Almost any surfacing material that's readily available and inexpensive will do. If you already have grass, you may decide to use that for your walkways — it's soft underfoot, and a gentle ribbon of green can act as a great foil for your ebullient borders. Many of the older cottage gardens simply used a path of compacted earth supplemented with wood and coal

---

❧ Climbing Vines for Arches

The walled gardens of the early Victorian gentry almost always had areas where the villagers could peep through on their Sunday afternoon walks (often a gate, or even specially constructed portholes) to gaze at the grand borders within. Before long, the cottagers were emulating this idea, and often archways would serve to support flowering vines or climbing vegetables, while at the same time framing a particularly picturesque view.

ANNUALS
Hyacinth bean — *Lablab purpureus* (syn. *Dolichos lablab*)
Moonflower — *Ipomoea alba*
Morning glory cultivars — *Ipomoea tricolor*
Scarlet runner bean — *Phaseolus coccineus*
Spanish flag — *Ipomoea lobata* (syn. *Mina lobata*)
Sweet pea — *Lathyrus odorata*

PERENNIALS
Clematis — Many species and cultivars — Hardiness variable
❦ Dutchman's pipe — *Aristolochia macrophylla* — Zones 5–8
Five-leaf akebia — *Akebia quinata* — Zones 5–9
Hardy kiwi vine — *Actinidia kolomikta* 'Arctic Beauty' — Zones 4–8
Honeysuckle — *Lonicera* species and cultivars — Hardiness variable
❦ Moonseed — *Menispermum canadense* — Zones 4–8, Fruit poisonous
Perennial sweet pea — *Lathyrus latifolius* 'White Pearl' — Zones 4–9
Porcelain berry — *Ampelopsis brevipedunculata* 'Elegans' — Zones 4–8
Climbing roses — *Rosa* species and cultivars — Hardiness variable
Japanese wisteria — *Wisteria floribunda* and cultivars — Zones 4–10
❦ = native

Informally laid brick provides a stable, durable pathway surface through this heady floral display. Pathways should do more than just direct you through the garden — they must also serve as functional access routes for seasonal maintenance and upkeep.

cinders as a surface, and this can be a good option if you're unsure of what you want to install permanently, or if you're still collecting pennies for the yellow brick road you contemplate building one day. A word of caution — a dirt pathway can quickly turn into a quagmire if you live in an area of high rainfall.

Some homeowners will opt for gravel paths, but they must be edged with wood or bricks to prevent the gravel from spilling into the beds, and *vice versa*. It's hard to shovel snow off a gravel path so it's best for pathways that won't be used in winter. Colored gravel always seems to work better in cottage gardens than gray gravel. The gray tones frequently appear harsh and sterile in a cottage garden, although they work wonderfully well in more formal situations. My other quarrel with gravel is that it requires regular weeding, and it also needs replacing every few seasons as it gradually sinks into the soil. Worst of all, cats (and here I include my own beloved Oliver) seem to think that gravel surfaces are nothing more or less than feline public conveniences, leading to some indelicate clean-up detail for the unfortunate homeowner.

Bricks, flagstone and pavers are all suitable materials for permanent surfaces. The trick here is not to combine too many types of materials. If you start with limestone flags, don't switch to granite halfway through. It's best to decide early on what your color (or range of colors) will be. If you start out with gray tones, stick with them — likewise, if you like stone of a reddish hue, don't start mixing in material peppered with purple quartz. The best approach is to try to use materials indigenous to your area. Where I live, there is a ready supply of Credit Valley or Wiarton flagstone. If I purchase either of these materials, I know I'm not paying for long-distance hauling and transport, and I have the added peace of mind that the stone I'm using is compatible with my local soil, since native soil is always largely derived from the underlying parent rock.

It's also wise to try to match the color and texture of your pathway with that of your house. If your home is constructed of red brick, using red brick as a pathway surface will help to connect the two spaces. If your house is constructed of wood, you may opt for large wooden rounds fabricated from the trunks of mature trees. Most importantly, no matter which surface material you eventually choose for your pathway, make sure that it's wide enough for your wheelbarrow to pass through with ease. It will save you a great deal of frustration in the future!

OTHER FEATURES

While many English cottage gardens contain defunct water wells and farm outbuildings, it's unlikely that these will be present in North American gardens. Nevertheless, North American gardens often contain garden sheds or garages that can serve as the perfect staging for climbing vines and window boxes or the ideal backdrop for a garden bench. Even if you don't have a permanent structure like a shed in your garden, there's a great deal of scope for extra ornamentation in the cottage garden which will greatly contribute to an authentic feel, without rendering it Disney-esque. Containers can be arrayed liberally throughout the garden without an eyebrow being raised. Colorful annuals and tender perennials beg to be festooned about willy-nilly for continuous bloom, and again, the simplest containers provide the best staging. I have a predilection for terra cotta, but you must be vigilant about watering if you choose a container that is as porous as these clay-based beauties. Using a container soil mix with water-absorbing polymers will alleviate your irrigation duties by about half.

A simple sundial may not be absolutely authentic to the cottage garden, but providing it's not overly flamboyant, it can add considerable intrigue and interest to the garden. As well, it preserves a real and poignant link to the days of yore, long before everybody's wrists began sporting glorified computer chips, capable of advising us of the local time in Kuala Lumpur. Bird feeders and baths also aren't visually distracting, and our avian friends will help keep populations of destructive insects low, although they'll likely help themselves to some of your produce as reimbursement for their efforts on your behalf.

Benches of wood and stone have long been fixtures in cottage gardens and are easy to construct or purchase pre-assembled. They are especially fitting structures on which to perch after a prolonged day of gardening. Experiment with different vantage points throughout the garden for at least one growing season before you decide on a permanent spot for sitting down and relaxing. There is a tremendous satisfaction to be had from surveying the day's handiwork from a semi-reclining position. Be forewarned, however, that this is likely to be a solitary pleasure, since only the steward of the garden will be capable of recounting the million and one chores satisfactorily completed.

Contrary to popular opinion, gardening isn't a spectator sport, and the only individuals who will derive a genuine sense of fulfillment will be the ones who hurl themselves headfirst into the midst of nature's fickle skirmish.

Horticulturist Judith Adam softens the edges of her driveway with terra cotta flower pots and wicker baskets lined with plastic. Just a few containers can make all the difference, transforming harsh edges into lush curves.

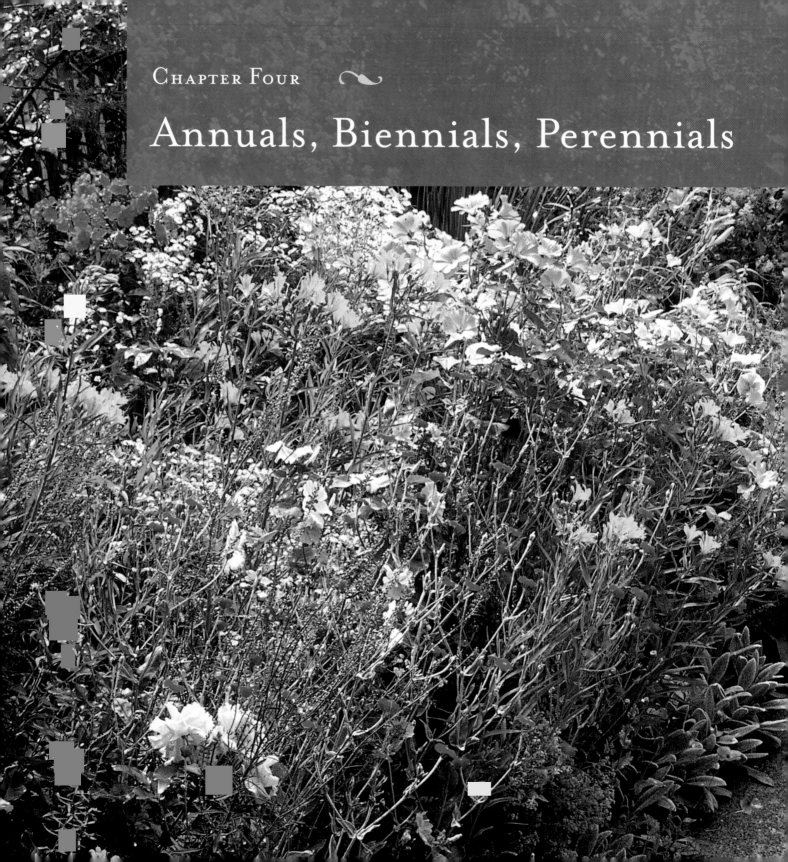

CHAPTER FOUR

Annuals, Biennials, Perennials

FLOWERING PLANTS ARE LIKELY to be the dominant feature in most North American cottage gardens. These plants can be divided into three main categories: annuals, biennials and perennials. Most annuals and biennials are easy to grow from seed. Annuals will flower, set seed and die in one season, while biennials will usually only produce foliage in their first year, and in the second, flower, set seed and die. Perennials can be either long-lived like peonies, or short-lived like many of the columbines (*Aquilegia* spp.). In theory anyway, perennials should live for at least three years — most of course, live much longer or set sufficient seed to ensure their long-term presence in the garden.

In recent years, many serious gardeners have snubbed annuals and biennials in favor of exclusively perennial borders, perhaps as a reaction to the dominance of annual bedding plants in post-World War II North America. Like so many others of my generation, I have childhood memories of mucky-colored red and white petunias in dead straight rows, planted in dead straight beds along the dead straight driveway. It had such an effect on me that I've only started growing petunias again in the last two years, and certainly never in straight lines. Nevertheless, every cottage garden should leave ample room for annuals. They take over beautifully from the bulbs once they've finished, and most of them provide bloom all season long, helping to link together the more sporadic blooms of the perennials. Transplant extra seedlings to containers, where they will look terrific as they fill out.

*Cottage gardens should never look contrived, and the best way to avoid this pitfall is to blend together as many colors, shapes and textures as possible. Notice how the gray leaves of rose campion (*Lychnis coronaria*) are skillfully utilized as a neutral edging while their hot-pink blooms augment the boisterous display above.*

Annuals

WHILE ALL ANNUALS flower, set seed and die in one season, it's important to remember that "hardy annuals" (like love-in-a-mist and opium poppies) can be depended on to furnish your garden with seedlings for years to come. On the other hand, "tender annuals" (like *Salpiglossis* and some morning glories) must be re-seeded every spring if their brilliant blooms are to be enjoyed during the dog days of summer. Here are several of my favorites.

Love-in-a-mist

Nigella damascena

ALTHOUGH NATIVE TO southern Europe and North Africa, love-in-a-mist is a fundamental cottage garden plant. John Gerard, author of the famous *Herball,* mentions that he had five kinds of *Nigella* growing at his Holborn garden, so it is a plant with a long and distinguished provenance and is one of those species that have almost come to be regarded as a native Brit. It's quite likely that at least a few of Gerard's specimens would have been *N. damascena*'s close cousin, *N. sativus* or black cumin.

Still widely used as a culinary spice in Middle Eastern and Indian cooking, during Elizabethan times the seeds of black cumin were commonly employed as a relish and stimulant to the taste buds. Botanist William Turner (one-time chaplain and physician to the Duke of Somerset) mentions it in his herbal of 1568, which was, in fact, dedicated to the Queen.

He's careful to add, however, that the seeds of *N. damascena* have no culinary value, and indeed this is true — the beauty is in the plant itself — no more and no less.

Many gardeners grow love-in-a-mist as much for the delicate, feathery foliage (the "mist") as for the blooms, but this is a mistake, since the species possess some truly stunning shades of blue as well as pink, white and purple. A hardy annual, it is best sown from seed directly where it is to flower, either in mid-autumn or late winter for bloom the next spring and summer. It tends toward taproots rather than fibrous roots, so it's best not to attempt transplanting *Nigella*. Fortunately, it's another prolific self-seeder and can be depended upon to produce four to five generations of healthy offspring. After this period of time, new plants will produce smaller blooms in muddy shades, so I usually rip everything out by about year four, often re-seeding the area with a different cultivar.

Cultivars of *Nigella damascena*

'Blue Midget' — A dwarf form (height to 10"/25 cm) suitable for edging or containers

'Cambridge Blue' — Double blue flowers on long stems, the best variety for bouquets

'Dwarf Moody Blue' — The shortest cultivar of all (8"/20 cm) with flowers that open purple and fade to sky blue

'Mulberry Rose' — A large-flowered variety whose light pink petals age to a deep rose

'Oxford Blue' — Double flowered, and the darkest blue of any cultivar

These days, flower arrangers are often the only gardeners that bother with this plant, not only because it makes a long-lasting cut flower, but also for its curiously ornamental seed pods, which are rounded, bulbous affairs, topped with small horns. These appendages may account for one of the other common names of *N. damascena*: devil-in-the-bush.

Love-in-a-mist is especially useful in the cottage garden. Because of its diaphanous form, it never crowds out other plants, it simply stretches out its slender arms and embraces its neighbors. If seedlings become too crowded, be ruthless and thin them out — you'll be rewarded with superior, more floriferous plants as a result. The notion of being unable to pull out "babies" is sentimentalism gone horribly wrong. Nature invariably snuffs out its own weaklings eventually, but in the garden, we have to be prepared to speed up the process. Intervention, in the form of removing genetically inferior plants, is the only way that the real gems can be isolated and then propagated. Select only the best.

The first group of *N. damascena* cultivars that I ever grew were the 'Persian Jewels' series. These plants come in a colorful array of blue, violet, rose and white flowers. They also seem to be the most robust and long-lived, with the 'Miss Jekyll' series following a close second. 'Miss Jekyll' has double the number of petals of the other cultivars and is therefore somewhat showier, although these strains can be difficult to obtain in any color other than light blue.

The intricate form of love-in-a-mist is unique among the hardy annuals. In spite of its delicate appearance, this plant is as tough as old boots and a single sowing will guarantee several generations of abundant bloom. While it's still in full flower, the enlarging horn-like structures of the seed pods are already in evidence.

Name: Love-in-a-mist *Nigella damascena*
Height: To 18" (45 cm)
Exposure: Sun to part sun
Blooming period: Summer
Soil: Ordinary well-drained garden soil. Water-logged conditions will promote root rot.
Companions: Lovely with lavender (*Lavandula angustifolia*) and culinary sage (*Salvia officinalis*)
Special notes: Seed can be re-sown throughout the summer for successional blooming

Morning glory

Convolvulus tricolor and
Ipomoea tricolor

IF YOU HAD TOLD me a decade ago that I'd ever end up writing a section in praise of morning glories, and 'Heavenly Blue' in particular, I'd have thought you were crazy. Morning glories weren't considered very highbrow back then, especially for an aspiring horticulturist. When I did begin growing them, I stuck to the rarer species and hard-to-get cultivars, many of them bordering on the bizarre, and for the most part not particularly salient when all was said and done. Luckily, times have changed, and so have I. Now I grow at least four different morning glory cultivars every summer, and they are always among the most arresting plants in sight, with the added benefit of providing the vertical accents essential to any successful garden. Morning glories deserve a place in all gardens, but especially in the cottage garden.

The common name of morning glory is generally reckoned to include the plants of two different genera, those of *Convolvulus* (native to Europe) and *Ipomoea* (native to South America), although both are members of the Convolvulaceae family. While this is probably of interest only to botanical taxonomists, the two groups do behave slightly differently. Being an important food source, *Ipomoea batatas* (sweet potato) was likely the first of the Ipomoeas to get to England (in the early 1620s), although it never caught on as a staple food the way it did in much of the western hemisphere. It is interesting to note that a mutation of the sweet potato with black leaves has been isolated and given the cultivar name

of 'Blackie' and is now a popular trailing container plant, producing supposedly edible tubers with a remarkably unpalatable appearance.

Convolvulus, on the other hand, was well known to cottagers, but unhappily as the vigorous pest bindweed (*Convolvulus arvensis*). The main difference between the two classes of morning glory is that Ipomoeas are usually energetic climbers that tend to flower later in the season, while *Convolvulus* species can be both climbers and bushy ramblers and generally flower five to six weeks before *Ipomoea*. Both types will continue to bloom until the first frosts of autumn.

More important to gardeners is what these plants have in common. The flowers of both open early in the morning and usually close by about noon. Most gardeners think that this behavior is related to light levels, but in fact, it has to do with temperature. Morning glories close when the sun gets high, because it just gets too hot for their pollinators to be out and about. Why entice midday insects into the folds of their brilliant blooms, when they'll be useless for procreational purposes? Nature never squanders anything—especially pollen and nectar—it takes too much energy to produce, so when the temperature gets too high, the plants close up shop for the day. This is the reason that morning glory flowers stay open much longer on cool cloudy days, as well as at the end of the season when crisp autumn temperatures deceive them into staying open much later than they normally would.

The other thing that all morning glories love is poor soil. Never fertilize them, especially with a solution containing nitrogen (the first number on the label). If you do, you'll be rewarded with rampant vegetative growth, but you can forget about flowers. To provide the ideal soil for morning glories, leave several patches of soil unamended with compost or manure, and plant the morning glories out in that area. Seedlings are very sensitive to cool temperatures and can be set back weeks if they're planted out too early. Wait until the ground is really warm, usually a week to ten days after it's safe to plant out tomatoes. With a steady supply of moisture while they're becoming established, a full sun location, and something to scramble up, you'll find yourself a morning glory *aficionado* in no time.

There are hundreds of morning glory varieties to choose from, many having recently been brought back from the edge of extinction. Keep your eyes peeled for these heirloom varieties, and be sure to collect the seed and pass some of it on to gardening friends.

Probably the best known of all morning glories is *Ipomoea tricolor* 'Heavenly Blue' in spite of its being, surprisingly, quite a recent introduction. Its prototype 'Blue Star' was frequently employed in gardens to cover up the outhouse exterior, which it did quite quickly and effectively. On the down side, though, it never bloomed until the very end of the season, and it flowered so early in the morning (about 4 AM) that no one ever had a chance to appreciate its floral attributes. In 1931 enter a Colorado gardener

*The rich color of 'Heavenly Blue' morning glories is hard to beat, but nevertheless this **Ipomoea** tricolor cultivar (first raised in 1931) has subsequently produced some much sought-after offspring. Resist the urge to fertilize these vigorous vines — they prefer a very lean diet! As happy in a container as in the open ground, it is seen here with passion flower (**Passiflora** caerulea).*

named Clarke, who selected a free-flowering mutant with large sky-blue flowers that bloomed in 90 days from seed, rather than the usual 120. 'Heavenly Blue' was born.

Many of today's more sought-after morning glories are subsequent mutations of Clarke's 'Heavenly Blue'. The well-known pure white 'Pearly Gates' introduced in 1942 is a mutation of 'Heavenly Blue', and the much rarer tie-dyed blossoms of 'Flying Saucers' (introduced in 1960) is itself only a mutant of 'Pearly Gates'. You can easily see how incestuous it all is, and why not even the most accomplished gardeners should ever be permitted to turn up their noses at 'Heavenly Blue', considering its magnificent descendants. I like to plant morning glories fairly densely to ensure a good show, and unlike so many plants, they don't object to crowded quarters.

The next set of morning glories to consider are those of the *Convolvulus* tribe. In spite of the fact that this group is responsible for several noxious weeds, it also contains some excellent garden subjects. The first that comes to mind is *Convolvulus tricolor* 'Royal Ensign', sometimes sold as 'Blue Ensign'. Deep blue, almost royal purple margins give way to a brilliant white that leads the eye down to the golden throat. The color of these plants is so vivid that it makes them difficult to photograph. Even with high-speed film, the blue is so intense that it often bleeds beyond its legitimate margins, giving the plant an almost artificial appearance.

'Royal Ensign' is a dwarf variety of morning glory with a bushy form and a consummate ability to insinuate itself among its neighbors, weaving in and out of their more defined outlines — the perfect "filler" plant. Like all morning glories, it is a tender annual in most of North America, and as such can be an unreliable self-seeder. The best approach is to start plants indoors and move them outside when it's really warm, disturbing their roots as little as possible. Just a few plants can fill in large areas without ever choking out nearby flora. 'Royal Ensign' grows between 12 and 18 inches (30 and 45 centimeters) high with a similar spread, and unlike so many annuals, it will continue blooming all summer long without ever requiring deadheading. A lesser known but equally spectacular plant is 'Red Ensign', similar in every respect to 'Royal Ensign', but with striking wine-red flowers. Both plants are long-time cottage garden residents, requiring the barest minimum of care, while rewarding the gardener with dependably breathtaking displays.

The other *Convolvulus* that I'd loath to be without is the vigorously self-seeding *C.* 'Star of Yelta'. Initially I suspected that 'Yelta' was a misspelling of Yalta, and that I was, in fact, growing a plant that hailed from the Ukraine, but it turns out that this cultivar was actually hybridized in Australia. Yelta is a village near Mildura on the northwestern borders of the state of Victoria, renowned not only for its citrus groves and vineyards, but also as a gateway to

---

❧ *Ipomoea* Cultivars Worth Trying

'Gypsy Bride' — Fully double carnation-like flowers with lavender-colored spots at the base of pure white petals

'Imperial Chocolate' — As the name implies, large chocolate brown flowers

'Platycodon Flowered' — Bright red or deep purple flowers with a pure white border

'Robe' — Burgundy blooms with a white "picotee" edge

'Wedding Bells' — Large lilac pink flowers introduced by morning glory hybridizer Darold Decker in 1961. Yet another mutation of 'Heavenly Blue'.

the Australian outback. Imagine what perfect conditions this sort of climate provides to morning glories! Hot and dry, just the way they like it.

Although technically a *Convolvulus*, 'Star of Yelta' behaves much more like a member of the *Ipomoea* genus. Rather than a dwarf bushy habit, 'Star of Yelta' is a rampant climber that could give any 'Heavenly Blue' a run for its money. An early and prolific bloomer, 'Star of Yelta' sports deep purple flowers with a star-like pink center. Lately I've taken to growing jumbo white gladioli up through the center of my wigwam-supported morning glories. Within a few weeks, 'Star of Yelta' have surrounded their quarry, binding them securely (and dispensing with the need for staking), without ever inflicting a stranglehold on them. The whole effect is quite lovely, if somewhat unorthodox. Remember, if anyone should ever sniff at your cozy display of morning glories, be sure to sniff right back at them. Only louder.

NAME: Morning glory *Convolvulus tricolor* and *Ipomoea tricolor*

HEIGHT: 8' (2.5 m) or more

EXPOSURE: Full sun

BLOOMING PERIOD: Summer to early autumn

SOIL: Performs best in poor or "lean" soil — never use nitrogen-based fertilizers

COMPANIONS: Tall gladioli or equally imposing plants such as shoo-fly (*Nicandra physalodes*)

SPECIAL NOTES: Some species and cultivars will self-seed freely

Opium poppy

 Papaver somniferum

BELIEVE IT OR not, it's true: they're at it again — trying to throw out the baby with the bath water. The opium poppy has recently become the subject of debate among (I assume) well-meaning drug enforcement officials. This seems particularly ludicrous for two reasons. In the first place, anyone who knows anything about medical botany knows that many common garden plants contain alkaloids that can seriously affect human health for good or ill. Second, an addict of opium or its derivatives is unlikely to have the capacity, let alone the patience, to grow opium poppies in sufficient quantities to maintain a serious drug habit for more than about a week. Furthermore, most drug enforcement agents wouldn't know a poppy from a peony. Enough said.

In spite of this distressing character assassination, the opium poppy remains one of the most popular of all cottage garden plants. A hardy annual, it self-seeds easily, providing rich, silky blooms of many casts, followed by the handsome seedpods so esteemed by flower arrangers. Chefs will be aware that our culinary "poppy seeds" are also derived from the opium poppy, although they don't contain any narcotic constituents. In other words, you won't get high from eating a poppy-seed bagel, but ironically enough, you might well fail a drug test.

Many gardeners don't even realize that the annual poppies they cherish are, in fact, opium poppies. Due to the stigma attached to the epithet *somniferum*, many cultivars became known by more discreet names such as "peony flowered" or 'paeoniflorum'. Still

Bakers love their seeds, flower arrangers love their seedpods, and gardeners love their elegant, silky blooms. Best seeded directly on the soil surface in early spring, opium poppies will self-sow for years once they're established. Be sure to experiment with different cultivars.

others simply adopted a cultivar name, leaving out the species altogether, such as *Papaver* 'White Cloud' or *P.* 'Hens and Chickens'. Call them what you will, they're all opium poppies, and they're all ravishingly beautiful.

It also seems terribly ungrateful of us to vilify a plant that has been used medicinally to alleviate pain since Neolithic times. Somewhere in our family trees, we all have forebears who were very thankful for the medicinal properties of this poppy species, making innumerable gruesome medical procedures considerably less excruciating. Even today, there is no more potent pain reliever for patients with terminal cancer than the morphia derivatives of the opium poppy.

In any case, gardeners can breathe a sigh of relief, since the seeds for opium poppies are widely available in both Canada and the United States. If you can't find a seed source, there's a good chance you can germinate the poppy seeds stocked in the spice rack at your grocery store. In warmer zones, seeds can be broadcast outdoors in late autumn for bloom the following spring and summer. In colder areas, wait until spring when the ground has thawed, and then sprinkle them on the soil surface in the same manner. No need to cover the seeds with soil. With either method, you will likely have to thin out the lettuce-leaved seedlings as they appear, leaving 6 to 8 inches (15 to 20 centimeters) between plants.

As with most hardy annuals, once you've introduced them into your garden, you'll have them forever, although you'll probably want to experiment with different cultivars as the years progress. All they require is plenty of sunlight. Once the plants have bloomed and set seed, the blue-green foliage will begin to yellow. Pull the plants out, and throw them on the compost heap, having saved some seed for next year. For a longer period of bloom, poppies may be sown several weeks apart early in the season, to provide a succession of flowering.

As we've already established, the Romans brought the opium poppy to Britain, but its history stretches much further back into time than that. Its use dates back at least as far as the Sumerians (5000 BC), and the first written account of the opium poppy comes to us from Mesopotamia where it's mentioned in the *Assyrian Herbal* (2000 BC). By the Middle Ages, most British herbals included the opium poppy (often referred to as the 'White Poppie'), with detailed instructions on how to extract the opium-rich latex (or sap). Even as late as 1931 when Mrs. Grieve published her encyclopedic *A Modern Herbal* (still in print), precise instructions are given regarding the collection and administration of opium poppy-based tonics.

About the worst thing that can reasonably be said about the opium poppy is that it was responsible for the Opium Wars fought between the British and the

Choice Opium Poppies for Cottage Gardens

'Danebrog' (Danish flag) – Single scarlet blooms with a broad white stripe across the center, 2 to 3' (60 to 90 cm) tall

'Hens and Chickens' – An unusual lavender-colored variety where the central pod (the hen) is surrounded by numerous small pods (the chickens). Excellent form for dried-flower arrangements, and reputedly especially high in narcotic alkaloids; height to 2' (60 cm)

'Peony Flowered Mix' – A wide range of colors on fully double blossoms; height to 3' (90 cm)

'Paeoniflorum Black' – Double black flowers followed by extra-large seed heads; height to 3' (90 cm)

'White Cloud' – The name says it all: Fluffy, billowing double white blooms; height to 3' (90 cm)

Chinese from 1839 to 1842. During a particularly ugly period in British history, opium was exported into China from British India in exchange for gold and silver, which in turn were used to buy tea and silk for the British market, exploiting two countries for the price of one. The by-product of this deplorable practice was that millions of Chinese citizens became addicted to opium, causing serious social and medical repercussions. It wasn't until 1917 when the Allies needed all the opium they could get their hands on for use in army field hospitals that the British voluntarily abolished this immoral trade.

NAME: Opium poppy *Papaver somniferum*
HEIGHT: 2 to 3' (60 to 90 cm)
EXPOSURE: Sun to part sun
BLOOMING PERIOD: Summer
SOIL: Average to rich
COMPANIONS: Good with similarly sized bellflowers (*Campanula* species) or among leafy vegetables (arugula, lettuce, radicchio, spinach, Swiss chard)
SPECIAL NOTES: Most easily grown by direct seeding in the spring — transplanting is difficult

Salpiglossis

 Painted tongue, Velvet flower

IT'S NOTHING SHORT of a crime against nature that salpiglossis isn't more widely grown. A member of the Solanaceae or nightshade family and a close relative of the petunia, *Salpiglossis sinuata* has somehow acquired the unenviable reputation of being difficult to grow. Let me assure you that nothing could be further from the truth, and having grown it once, you'll never look back.

Salpiglossis come in a veritable rainbow of colors. Frequently, a single flower will be made up of many hues with a contrasting eye, and wonderful venation etched boldly on every petal. The velvety flowers have been compared to stained-glass windows, and indeed, the effect is very similar.

Salpiglossis is a relatively new introduction to cottage gardens, and like so many New World plants, it made its way to Britain as a result of political change and upheaval more than anything else. The Spanish and Portuguese empires in South and Central America began to crumble in the first quarter of the nineteenth century, and in just eight years (between 1816 and 1824), Argentina, Brazil, Chile, Colombia, Costa Rica, Ecuador, Guatemala, Mexico, Peru and Venezuela all achieved independence, much to Britain's delight. Up until this time, British exploration and trade in these regions had been at the mercy of the Spanish and Portuguese bureaucrats, who were loath to let the English gain a foothold. With independence, however, these restrictions were lifted. This meant that for the first time, plant collectors were given free rein to explore these new lands, and as they did wherever they roamed, British botanists immediately began sending plant samples home to growers in England.

Although tropical plants from Brazil and other countries within ten degrees of the equator were suitable only for indoor greenhouse cultivation, Argentina and Chile, as well as the mountainous areas of Colombia, Ecuador, Mexico and Peru, were absolutely teeming with new plants that could cope with the British climate.

One of the earliest plant collectors to forge his way through the native terrain of South America was Dr. John Gillies. Initially he set up camp at Mendoza, a city situated in the southern Andean foothills, just on the Argentine side of the Chilean border sometime in the early 1820s. It was on these dry, rocky slopes that English eyes first clapped on *Salpiglossis sinuata*, and Gillies immediately sent seeds and specimens back to Britain. The new plant was quickly adopted by gardening enthusiasts, and we can assume it made its way into cottage gardens a short time later, probably about 1840.

How then did a plant accustomed to such inhospitable conditions ever come to be regarded as difficult to grow? Many authorities report that it dislikes heat and cold. Being a half-hardy (or tender) annual, it does dislike cold, but heat is never a problem. Plants flower prolifically during hot spells, but require deadheading in order to continue to produce new buds; perhaps that is how the confusion over heat tolerance first arose. To make matters worse, one specialist will tell you to keep the plants evenly moist, while another warns against overwatering. It's at this point that gardeners must use their common sense and remember that this plant hails from an area where their environmental circumstances can best be described as spartan.

Although I've occasionally seen salpiglossis seedlings for sale at nurseries, most gardeners grow

Pictured here with lavender (Lavandula angustifolia *'Munstead'*) *and vervain* (Verbena officinalis), *it is easy to see why the blooms of salpiglossis have been compared with stained-glass windows. This flamboyant relative of the petunia is considered difficult to grow in some circles, but in fact the opposite is true.*

their own plants from seed. This is the only part of the operation that some people may find challenging as the seeds are very small and require careful handling. They also need to be started indoors rather than seeding them *in situ* outside, where they are to bloom. Sprinkle the seed on the surface of a sterile seed-starting mixture, and small plants will begin to appear in two to three weeks. Light levels aren't important during the germination process (in fact, they prefer darkness), but once germination occurs, they should be moved into a high light situation. As with other tender annuals, harden them off outdoors gradually, and don't plant them out until the ground is sufficiently warm — usually about the same time that it's safe to plant out tomatoes.

Like Vita Sackville-West, I'm inclined to agonize about whether it's worth the trouble to grow tender annuals since they lack the ability to self-seed from year to year. Invariably, however, when the salpiglossis appear for the first time in their full glory (usually toward the end of June), my qualms are instantly laid to rest.

Writing in 1937, Vita also complained that "salpiglossis" is not a particularly euphonious name, and while I'm reluctant to lock horns with such an impressive literary figure, I have to disagree. I think the name sounds tremendously *Through the Looking Glass* and can hardly believe that it isn't a Lewis Carroll original. Vita's dearest desire was that the plant should acquire a common name within the next century, and to a degree her wish has come true. Both painted tongue and velvet flower have come to be recognized as common names, but neither has ever enjoyed the wide usage of the original botanical name of *salpiglossis*, Greek for a "trumpet" (*salpinx*) and "tongue" (*glossa*). Fortunately, we've avoided the all-too-tempting alternative option of "trumpet-tongue" as a common name!

Salpiglossis makes a good cut flower, and regular culling for indoor arrangements will help the plant assume a bushier form, while lengthening its life expectancy. Many of the recent cultivars have been developed for use as container plants, but this idea is anything but new. The Victorians loved to cultivate salpiglossis as a greenhouse plant, to be brought into the main house for mid-winter bloom. Writing in 1863, Edward Sprague Rand Jr. notes in his best-selling *Flowers for the Parlor and Garden* that salpiglossis "is properly a green-house plant, but does well started in a hot-bed in April, and transplanted into a highly-manured sandy loam." He goes on to say that "it may be kept in the greenhouse for years, if not allowed to seed." While he's correct about not letting plants go to seed, the manure part is sheer fantasy. The best results can

---

∿ Salpiglossis for Cottage Gardens

Salpiglossis sinuata seeds are available in several mixes or "series," each emphasizing a different range of colors or growth habits. Choose the one that suits your purposes best.

'Bolero' mix — A wide color range on large, vigorous plants, 2 to 3' (60 to 90 cm) high. An excellent choice for the salpiglossis novice.
'Casino' mix — Every imaginable color combination on medium-sized plants, 18 to 24" (45 to 60 cm) high
'Gloomy Rival' — Who could resist a name like that? Flowers have an unusual blue-gray background with brown venation and a chocolate-colored center. Height to 30" (75 cm).
'Kew Blue' — Clear blue flowers with conspicuous venation
'Royal Chocolate' — Deep maroon to black flowers with a contrasting yellow eye. Plants are compact and dwarf-sized, making them especially suitable for containers.

be achieved by growing it in very average garden soil in full sun and dry conditions. Lately I've taken to growing it in a nutrient-starved herb garden with intentionally poor soil, where the only water it receives is from the sky. Here it associates happily with vervain, lavender and artemisia, whose gray foliage helps to chill out the intense, dramatic colors of its blossoms. Fussy it ain't!

NAME: Painted tongue *Salpiglossis sinuata*
HEIGHT: 2 to 3' (60 to 90 cm)
EXPOSURE: Full sun
BLOOMING PERIOD: Summer
SOIL: Ordinary to poor garden soil
COMPANIONS: Best with "simple" neighbors such as silver artemisias and feverfew (*Tanacetum parthenium*)
SPECIAL NOTES: A half-hardy annual — plants must be started from seed or purchased as transplants each year

❧ High-performance Annuals for the Cottage Garden

In addition to the plants we've discussed, be sure to consider the following 10 annuals when planning your cottage garden. A few weeks after planting, they'll look as if they had been there forever. Notice how many are from the western hemisphere!

Browallia (*Browallia speciosa*) from South America
Cosmos (*Cosmos bipinnatus*) from Mexico
❀ Five-spot (*Nemophila maculata*) from North America
❀ Flowering tobacco (*Nicotiana sylvestris*) from North America
Heliotrope (*Heliotropium arborescens*) from South America
Nasturtium (*Tropaeolum majus*) from South America
Night-scented stocks (*Matthiola incana*) from Europe
Pansy (*Viola x wittrockiana*) derived from hybridized *Viola* species
Spider flower (*Cleome hassleriana*) from South America
Verbena bonariensis (actually a tender perennial, but behaves like a hardy annual) from South America
❀ = native

Biennials

BIENNIAL PLANTS LIVE for two years. During their first year they typically form a leafy green rosette, and in their second year they will flower, set seed and die. As with annuals, some biennials (such as foxgloves) will self-seed readily, while others (such as Canterbury bells) will succeed best if fresh seed is sown indoors each spring. Making up a much smaller group of plants than annuals or perennials, biennials are nevertheless essential components of the cottage garden.

them. Occasionally, second-year plants can be found at garden centers, but by this time they will have developed a fairly extensive taproot, so be extra careful during the transplanting process.

Canterbury bells are hardy to at least zone 5 and also do well at high altitudes, providing the growing season is not less than 50 days. The seed of Canterbury bells is quite small, so sprinkle it carefully over a sterile soilless mix — no need to cover the seeds with soil. Germination should occur within two weeks, and once the plants have started to form their first-year basal rosettes, they can be safely planted outside where they will flower the following year.

Perhaps one of the reasons that Canterbury bells aren't grown more extensively is due to their biennial habit. Many of the most beautiful garden plants fall into this category, but a lot of them self-seed

Canterbury bells

 Campanula medium

THE PASTEL HUES of Canterbury bells are among the loveliest blooms of early summer, and it's a shame that more gardeners don't grow them. A true biennial, Canterbury bells can be coaxed into bloom during one growing season in Britain if the seeds are started indoors during the winter, but this method doesn't work well in North America.

The best time for us to sow seeds is just about the time we start moving other seedlings outdoors, toward the end of spring. This fits most gardeners' schedules, since the first part of the season is usually the busiest, so get your spring chores taken care of first. It is possible to start seeds outside, but you'll have better success if you begin them indoors in peat pellets or soil blocks, where you can keep an eye on

Canterbury Bell Cultivars

'Bells of Holland' — Dwarf plants bear single blooms in a variety of colors; height to 18" (45 cm)

'Calycanthema' — (also known as 'Cup and Saucer') — An interesting variety that won the Award of Merit in 1889. Coming in a variety of colors, each bell (cup) is surrounded by a flat calyx (saucer) of the same color. Flowers may be double or single; height to 30" (75 cm)

'Chelsea Pink' — A novelty form that really will flower in three months from seed. Makes an excellent container plant; height to 15" (37 cm)

'Dwarf Musical Bells' — Especially showy and very prolific, this variety comes in a wide range of colors; height to 18" (45 cm)

around the garden, behaving almost like hardy annuals. Unfortunately, Canterbury bells don't self-seed reliably. In addition, by mid-summer the spent blossoms necessary for seed formation look quite forlorn for rather longer than most gardeners can tolerate. Removing spent blossoms as they fade will often produce a second flush of buds, prolonging the duration of flowering. Nevertheless, if you want Canterbury bells in your garden every year without fail, you will likely have to seed them yourself annually. Once your Canterbury bells have finished blooming, discard last year's plants, amend the soil with organic matter, and plant out your fresh crop of seedlings for next year's blossoms.

A native of southern Europe, Canterbury bells have been a cottage garden plant since early times, and in Britain at least, they have long been associated with things religious. Many authorities maintain that *Campanula medium* was first dedicated to St. Augustine, who began his conversion of the English in 597. Having baptized King Ethelbert of Kent, St. Augustine was subsequently granted the see of Canterbury as Archbishop of the English. Very likely, Canterbury bells grew as plentifully in Kent then as they do today, and perhaps this is how the relationship originated.

Five hundred years later, in his *Canterbury Tales*, Chaucer depicts the yearly pilgrimage to the shrine of St. Thomas à Becket at Canterbury, "the holy blissful martyr for to seek." In his account, we observe his cast of characters riding southeast and doubtless ringing the bells that adorned their horses' harnesses. Conventional wisdom asserts that it was for these bells that the blue, bell-shaped flowers that grew so plentifully in the Kentish woods at that time of year were named. The plants' association with St. Augustine seems to have been dropped by this time, and he was remembered primarily for

An unreliable self-seeder, the blooms of Canterbury bells are well worth the extra effort it takes to seed a few cell packs toward the end of spring once you've transplanted the bulk of your other seedlings outdoors. Here they mingle happily with the hot pink blooms of rose campion (Lychnis coronaria), a short-lived perennial.

NAME: Canterbury bells *Campanula medium*
HEIGHT: To 30" (75 cm)
EXPOSURE: Sun to part sun
BLOOMING PERIOD: Summer
SOIL: Ordinary to rich garden soil
COMPANIONS: Hardy geranium species and cultivars do well around the base of these plants as does sea lavender (*Limonium latifolium*)
SPECIAL NOTES: Assiduous deadheading may produce a second flush of flowers

cursing the people of Rochester after they threw fish heads at him. He swore that from then on, any children born in that city would have tails, and for centuries it was believed that all its citizens were so endowed.

Add another 500 years to the equation, and the water becomes even muddier. By 1597 when Gerard's *Herball* appeared, he considered that Canterbury bells referred to the nettle-leaved bellflower (*Campanula trachelium*) and that the *Campanula medium* of gardens was properly called Coventry bells. In the end though, it appears that the larger, more attractive plant was eventually accorded the place name with the greater status, and *Campanula medium* has been known as Canterbury bells ever since.

Forget-me-not

Myosotis spp.

ONE OF THE BEST things about tulip time in the spring is that it coincides with the blooming of the forget-me-nots. This is one of those plants that even non-gardeners can not only recognize but name. Despite this widespread familiarity, however, few people really use them to their full potential. Forget-me-nots look best in association with other plants, and with tulips in particular. The dainty pale blue flowers make an ideal carpet for the statuesque tulip blooms, and regardless of their color combinations, they seem incapable of clashing.

Forget-me-nots belong to one of my favorite group of plants, the Borage family, and are widely distributed throughout the temperate zones of the world. Some are annuals or short-lived perennials, but most species behave in a true biennial manner. Different species can be used in different locations, and no matter where you garden, there's a forget-me-not for you.

The alpine forget-me-not (*Myosotis alpestris*) is hardy to zone 3 or 4 and can be grown up to about 10,000 feet (3,000 m) providing it's given some winter protection against the wind (evergreen boughs work nicely). If you have damp areas in your garden, the short-lived perennial water forget-me-not (*M. scorpioides*) will be the best choice for you. The most common garden form of forget-me-not across the rest of North America is the woodland forget-me-not (*M. sylvatica*) and its cultivars. All forget-me-not species are of easy culture and once established in the garden will self-seed for years. I like to introduce different seed strains every three to four years to keep the stock strong and to increase the variety of colors. In addition to the standard sky blue, forget-me-nots are also available in white, pink and a much darker blue.

Seeds may be scattered on the soil surface at

NAME: Forget-me-not *Myosotis* spp.
HEIGHT: To 14" (35 cm)
EXPOSURE: Sun to part shade
BLOOMING PERIOD: Spring
SOIL: Ordinary to rich garden soil
COMPANIONS: Perfect under tulips or combined with other spring flowers such as *Primula* spp. or ❧Rue anemone (*Anemonella thalictroides*)
SPECIAL NOTES: After flowers have faded, a ruthless thinning is generally required to prevent overcrowding, which can promote mildew

To my mind, forget-me-nots and tulips were made for one another. The aristocratic double late tulip 'Angelique'
(raised 1959) emerges from a sea of Myosotis; the elevated terra cotta pot sporting duplicate plant material lends height,
amounting to a stroke of whimsical cottage garden genius.

almost any time of year — there's no need to start them indoors. Most forget-me-not species appear to be equally happy in either sun or shade, as long as the shade isn't too dense. If a patch of forget-me-not becomes overgrown or begins to look ragged by midsummer, the plants can be easily pulled up and discarded, since the seed for the following season will already have been released.

Although "forget-me-not" would appear to be an old cottage garden appellative *extraordinaire*, it is, in fact, quite a recent name. Until the beginning of the nineteenth century, the plant was commonly known as scorpion grass in England and was used to treat insect bites (English scorpions being a rather scarce commodity).

No less a literary goliath than Samuel Taylor Coleridge (1772–1834) is credited with coining the name forget-me-not. Coleridge visited Germany from 1798–99, and it was there that he became acquainted with the Teutonic legend of the brave knight who drowned while trying to pick some forget-me-nots for his beloved on the banks of the Danube. Just before being dragged under by the swift current, the knight cried, "*Vergiss mich nicht*" or "Forget me not." Once back in England, Coleridge began contributing poems (some of his best) to the *Morning Post*, and it was in that newspaper that "The Keepsake" was first published in 1802.

> . . . Nor can I find, amid my lonely walk
> By rivulet, or spring, or wet roadside
> That blue and bright-eyed flowerlet of
>   the brook,
> Hope's gentle gem, the sweet Forget-me-not!

∾ A Forget-me-not for Every Garden

ALPINE FORGET-ME-NOT (*Myosotis alpestris*)
'Pink Pearls' — Bright silver-pink flowers on a compact plant; height to 6" (15 cm)
'Rosylva' — Large deep pink flowers on a bushy, vigorous plant; 1997 Fleuroselect Gold Medal winner; height to 14" (35 cm)
'Royal Blue' — Quite a deep shade of blue on compact plants, especially good with tulips; height to 6" (15 cm)
'White Ball' — A good white variety (some varieties tend to be greeny-white); height to 6" (15 cm)

WATER FORGET-ME-NOT (*Myosotis scorpioides*)
'Mermaid' — Dark green leaves frame bright blue, yellow-eyed flowers; height to 9" (22.5 cm)
'Sapphire' — Jewel-blue flowers on a plant with a branched, bushy habit; height to 8" (20 cm)

WOODLAND FORGET-ME-NOT (*Myosotis sylvestris*)
'Ball Series' cultivars — Especially 'Blueball' (azure) and 'Snowball' (white). Compact plants; height to 6" (15 cm)
'Blue Basket' — Deep blue flowers; height to 12" (30 cm)
'Blue Bird' — Introduced in 1934; bright blue flowers; height to 10" (25 cm)
'King Henry' — An ancient strain, very close to the species form with sky-blue flowers; height to 12" (30 cm). One of my favorites.
'Ultramarine' — Deep indigo blue flowers on a compact plant; height to 6" (15 cm)
'Victoria Series' — Dwarf variety introduced in 1928 and available in white, pink and blue strains; height to 4" (10 cm). 'Victoria Rose' is an especially bright pink form (some pink cultivars can look muddy from a distance).

An old English superstition asserts that forget-me-nots signify not only true love, but also constancy. To this end, the practice of friends exchanging plants on February 29 (each leap year) became popular during the Middle Ages. I'll add my own irrational two cents' worth at this point, and that is that forget-me-nots acquired as gifts from the garden of a dear friend always grow more robustly than those you raise yourself. Go figure.

Foxglove

Digitalis purpurea

I FIRST BECAME acquainted with foxgloves at about the age of three, courtesy of Beatrix Potter and *The Tale of Jemima Puddle-Duck*. Foxgloves have long been associated with foxes, perhaps because in the wild they tend to grow in places that foxes are likely to frequent. This fact wasn't lost on Beatrix Potter, herself an amateur naturalist. Who can forget the scene she sets when first introducing the foxes' character? "Jemima alighted rather heavily, and began to waddle about in search of a convenient dry nesting-place. She rather fancied a tree-stump amongst some tall foxgloves. But — seated on the stump, she was startled to find an elegantly dressed gentleman reading a newspaper."

The foxgloves that Potter was referring to were the common foxglove or *Digitalis purpurea*. While many foxgloves are perennial, *D. purpurea* tends to a strictly biennial habit, although occasionally a plant can be coaxed into blooming during its first year, or even into holding on for a third. Known in Britain

since Neolithic times, common foxglove has become naturalized across much of North America during the last two centuries. Foxgloves are one of the first really tall herbaceous plants to bloom in the late spring to early summer garden, adding much-needed height before other plants hit their stride. They can be grown in part shade to full sun. In addition to the range of colors found in the wild (white, pink and purple), cultivars may be had in maroon, apricot and pale yellow. Foxgloves make excellent cut flowers, although each individual bloom lasts only about six days. Cottagers used to add foxgloves to cut-flower bouquets or add foxglove "tea" to the vase water in order to extend the life of other flowers in the arrangement.

Despite the fact that foxgloves are available at most garden centers, you can have many more plants for a fraction of the price if you raise your own from seed. Foxgloves are not difficult to start from seed, but if you're attempting it for the first time, you may decide to begin the process indoors. Germination takes place in 10 to 14 days, at which

❧ A Foxglove by Any Other Name

Like all English plants that have been widely cultivated over the course of many centuries, *Digitalis purpurea* has a multitude of colorful local names:

Bloody man's fingers (Herefordshire)
Deadmen's bellows — i.e., "pillies" or penis (Northern England)
Dragon's mouth (Sussex)
Fairy fingers (Ireland)
Finger hut — a derivation of the German word for thimble: *fingerhut* (Devonshire)
Witch's thimble (Northumberland)

point the seedlings should be moved into an area with high light (but avoid the heat of a south-facing window — west- or east-facing is preferable). Harden off as usual, and plant outside after any danger of frost has passed.

Like all biennials, foxgloves usually spend their first year forming a leafy rosette and will bloom the second year. Hardy to zone 4, foxgloves grow from 3 to 7 feet (1 to 2 meters) depending on your location and the cultivar you select. Once established, they will self-seed freely, producing as many as two million seeds per plant. If your second generation is too successful, some thinning may be necessary to prevent the seedlings from crowding each other to death.

Some gardeners complain that they lose their foxgloves over the first winter, but this can easily be avoided. Foxgloves hate to be coddled — they're essentially a wild plant, capable of taking care of themselves. Never use water-soluble fertilizer on your plants, and likewise don't plant them in especially rich soil; that should be saved for heavy feeders. In their natural habitat, foxgloves grow in slightly acidic, nutrient-poor soil, so try to mimic these conditions as far as practical.

Another thing that can kill your foxgloves during the winter is water-logged soil. They require really efficient drainage to prevent rot around their crowns, so if you're in doubt, add some sand, grit or very fine gravel to the soil before installing them permanently. Finally, the third enemy of foxgloves is howling winter wind. In the first year, rosettes stay green throughout the winter, and excessive desiccation from wind may injure them beyond redemption. Try to choose a reasonably sheltered spot in your garden — against a fence or somewhere that snow collects. If all else fails, use the old evergreen bough method to provide a protective covering in the winter.

❦ *Digitalis purpurea* Cultivars

There are a large number of common foxglove cultivars available, but one word of caution. If you grow different types close to one another, they will probably cross-pollinate, and the resulting seedlings will be unlikely to come true to type.

'Alba' — Tall spires of pure white unspotted flowers — must be isolated to keep strain pure; height to 4' (120 cm)

'Campanulata' — An old mutant strain whereby the top flowers are united to form a single large bloom; height to 5' (1.5 m)

'Dwarf Sensation' — Rather than pendulous flowers, these are held horizontally. Less than 3' (90 cm) tall.

'Excelsior Hybrids' — Introduced about 1950, with a wide color range and horizontally held flowers borne all around the flower spike, rather than just on one side. Horticultural guru Graham Stuart Thomas disapproved of these new types, maintaining that the natural grace of the species had been destroyed. Height to 6' (180 cm).

'Foxy Hybrids' — Often behaves as an annual, blooming the first year; height to 3' (90 cm)

'Giant Shirley' — Large pink flowers developed by Reverend Henry Wilkes, who is also responsible for 'Shirley' poppies. Dates from the 1890s; height to 6 to 7' (1.8 to 2 m)

'Gloxinioides' — Hardly recognizable as a foxglove at all, this plant looks more like a gloxinia on steroids. An acquired taste; height to 7' (2 m)

Sutton's Apricot — Another Victorian cultivar with pinkish-orange flowers; height to 6' (180 cm)

Grown in cottage gardens from the early fifteenth century onwards, foxgloves are mentioned as being widespread in a list of plants that was compiled for Edward III (1312–77). The name foxglove has been attributed to the Saxon *folc's cleoff* (meaning fairies' bed), and indeed, the plant is richly associated with witchcraft, fairies and pixies in country lore. There seems little doubt, however, that the common name springs from the Old English *foxes glofa*, or foxglove. When it came time for Bavarian botanist Leonard Fuchs (of *Fuchsia* fame) to assign the plant a Latin name in 1542, he chose digitalis (from *digitus*) meaning finger, carrying the glove theme even further.

The common foxglove was used in folk medicine for centuries despite its toxicity, principally as a diuretic. This led an English doctor, William Withering, to conduct clinical tests on the plant, and in 1785 he published *Account of the Foxglove*. Withering's studies found that foxglove both strengthened and slowed the heart beat, enabling the kidneys and lungs to work more efficiently, thereby clearing the body of excess fluid. By conducting new research on an old herbal remedy, Withering had stumbled across an important medical breakthrough that many people still depend on today to keep them alive.

Name: Foxglove *Digitalis purpurea*

Height: To 5' (1.5 m) or more

Exposure: Part sun to shade

Blooming period: Late spring to summer

Soil: Best in well-drained ordinary garden soil

Companions: Terrific with *great lobelia (*Lobelia siphilitica*) and *Jacob's ladder (*Polemonium caeruleum*)

Special notes: For carefree propagation leave a few seed capsules on the plant to mature

It was also the detection of the medical properties of this plant (by a recognized scientist) that led to its introduction to North America. In 1787 Withering sent purple foxglove seeds to a doctor in New Hampshire, who subsequently sent seeds to a Boston physician in 1789. Over 200 years later, naturalized foxgloves look as much at home on our shores as they do on Britain's.

Hollyhock

Alcea rosea

THE HOLLYHOCK IS another flower that is best designated a biennial in North America, but is technically a short-lived perennial. Hardy to zone 3 and capable of growing as high as 10 feet (3 meters), hollyhocks represent one of the tallest plants in the cottage garden, and although many gardeners place them against walls and fences, they look equally glorious when left to their own devices to self-seed haphazardly around the garden.

All hollyhocks require a full-sun location with reasonably good garden soil. While the species tend to bloom in shades of white, pink, purple and yellow, cultivars are available in almost every color under the sun except blue, and flowers may be either single or double types. The tallest varieties will likely need staking, but if that isn't to your taste, dwarf varieties are available that are capable of supporting themselves.

Hollyhocks have fallen out of favor with many gardeners because they are prone to a disease called hollyhock rust. This disease first manifests itself as

Framed by a white picket fence, the tall spires of hollyhock paired with butterfly bush (Buddleja *spp.*, *syn.* **Buddleia**) *fairly scream "cottage garden." Prone to rust disease, these short-lived perennials are best treated as biennials. Cottage gardeners should also leave some space to experiment with the lesser-known fig-leaved hollyhock* (A. ficifolia).

small orange spots on the upper side of the leaves (these are actually the spores), and eventually badly infected leaves will drop off. Spraying with a sulfur-based fungicide before symptoms appear can be helpful, but once the disease takes hold, plants should be destroyed and thrown out (don't compost infected plant material). Picking off individual leaves or spraying with fungicide after the orange spots are present is useless. The rust parasites have already made their way deep into the vascular system of the plant where sprays can't penetrate.

This is the main reason that hollyhocks are treated as biennials. Older plants appear more susceptible to rust disease, and by propagating new stock each year and discarding second-year-old plants (which may have come into contact with rust spores), you will lessen the likelihood of rust gaining a foothold in your garden. Several strains of rust-resistant hollyhocks are now on the market, but even these tend to be better some years than others depending on local weather conditions,

which may or may not favor the proliferation of rust. All that being said, hollyhocks are a rugged bunch, and even if some plants get rust, the chances are good that you'll still be left with enough healthy plants for an impressive display.

Hollyhock seeds are relatively large and need to be covered with soil. Although plants will self-seed readily, I usually start some off indoors as an insurance policy, which also affords the opportunity to try new cultivars. Seedlings should be moved into the open ground fairly early in the season to avoid disturbing the long taproot that they quickly develop.

The origin of hollyhocks is somewhat uncertain, although it's generally agreed that they were first cultivated in Western China. How they got to England is another story. During the Crusades (commencing in 1096), two military orders were closely associated with bringing several new plants back to Britain, and it is the Knights Templars whom we must credit with the introduction of the hollyhock. The common name itself would seem to back up this

∾ Hollyhock Varieties

'Blackcurrant Whirl' – Dramatic, to the point of being over-the-top. The scrumptious color of blackcurrants swirled together with a dash of clotted cream. Semi-double; height to 8' (2.5 m)

'Chater's Double' – A widely-grown series in both bright colors and pastel shades. Fully double; height to 7' (2 m)

'East Coast Hybrids' – An old variety from the early 1930s, recently rescued from obscurity in the East Anglian village of Aldeburgh. Single blooms in every shade including black, slate gray, rust and copper; height to 8' (2.5 m)

'Indian Spring' – Introduced in 1939, single blooms of white, pink and primrose yellow; height to 6' (180 cm)

'Majorette' – A bushy, dwarf variety with fringed semi-double flowers in pastel shades; height to 3' (90 cm)

'Nigra' – One of my favorites, and reasonably rust resistant. A natural mutation isolated between 1800 and 1825, the single flowers are such a deep maroon that they look quite black. Height to 6' (180 cm).

'Powder Puff' Strains – Medium-sized plants with large double flowers in a good range of colors; height to 5' (1.5 m)

'Summer Carnival' – Double flowers that are produced much closer to the base of the flowering spike than on other cultivars. Primarily in shades of red and yellow; height to 6' (180 cm)

theory since "hollyhock" is a corruption of "holy oak," *holy* referring to the Holy Land where the Templars first found it, and *oak* referring (loosely) to the shape of the leaves. Hollyhocks were first mentioned in British manuscripts as far back as 1440 and would have appeared in cottage gardens at about the same time.

Like all members of the *Malva* (or mallow) family, hollyhocks contain starchy, mucilaginous constituents that were widely used in country medicine to sooth mucous membranes. It was for this purpose that the plant was introduced to North America by the Puritans in the first half of the seventeenth century. Nevertheless, it appears that Dutch settlers of the same period were growing the blowsy double forms simply as ornamentals, which no doubt the ultra-practical Puritans thought extremely improvident of them.

There is a renewed interest in saving heirloom varieties of hollyhock since many of them appear to be rust resistant and would be very useful in the breeding of new cultivars. Many modern gardeners also prefer the simple flower structure of the older varieties over the fussy pom-pom forms that made a comeback in the 1930s, after falling from favor after their heyday in the Victorian era. Whatever the case, you'll find that the height hollyhocks provide, coupled with their long season of bloom (often from early summer to first frosts), make them indispensable residents of the North American cottage garden.

Sweet William

Dianthus barbatus

SWEET WILLIAM SEEMS to me to be a victim of the class system. Most *Dianthus* enthusiasts start their excursion into pinks and carnations with this delightful short-lived perennial, but they frequently relinquish it when they become sophisticated enough to sport *Dianthus knappii* in their borders. Never mind, the horticultural *nouveaux riches* generally come back to them in the end, and in the meantime, it leaves more seed for the rest of us.

Sweet William is a cottage garden plant of old and, as is the case with so many of the plants we treat as biennials, the best bloom is to be had from two-year-old plants. Occasionally, precocious seedlings started indoors will produce some flowers the first season, and if they do, be sure to deadhead them. After they flower the second season, it's best to let the plants set seed and then toss them out. This approach sounds somewhat bloodthirsty, but it's the best way to ensure superior flowering.

Native to Eurasia and hardy to zone 3, Sweet Williams come in a variety of shades ranging from pure white to pink and red combinations. Unlike the rest of the *Dianthus* genera, Sweet Williams hold

NAME: Hollyhock *Alcea rosea*
HEIGHT: To 7' (2 m)
EXPOSURE: Sun to part sun
BLOOMING PERIOD: Summer to autumn
SOIL: Ordinary to rich garden soil
COMPANIONS: Works well alone or with spider flower (*Cleome hassleriana*) and garden phlox (*Phlox paniculata* and cultivars)
SPECIAL NOTES: Where rust disease is a problem, remove and destroy plants at the first sign of infection

many clusters of individual flowers per stem rather than just one, giving them the appearance of dwarf phlox. Best of all, their markings are exquisite—they may have dark or light contrasting bands, or fringed petals, or both—the variations are endlessly elegant.

To get off to a good start, begin your seeds indoors, then move them outside after hardening them off. Sweet William will grow in part shade to full sun, but it requires reasonably fertile, well-drained soil. Plants will thrive at elevations of up to 10,000 feet (3,000 meters), but instead of growing to their usual height of 12 to 18 inches (30 to 45 centimetres), they'll form low colorful mats of flowers.

There are several theories as to how this plant acquired its English label, and two of the oldest traditions link it to saints of the same name. The first is St. William of Aquitaine (died 812), who was a soldier in Charlemagne's army and who helped to chase the Saracens from France. The second was St. William of Rochester (Kent), but other than the fact that *Dianthus barbatus* grew profusely in the area, there doesn't seem to be a very strong connection. Yet another hypothesis suggests that it was named after William the Conqueror (1027–87) during the Norman conquest of England.

By 1597, when Gerard's *Herball* was first pub-

The exquisite markings of Sweet William appear to be endless, and they've been grown in English cottage gardens since the Dark Ages. Because the best blooms will be produced by two-year-old plants, it's not a bad idea to sow an extra cell pack or two every spring at about the same time you're thinking about a new generation of Canterbury bells.

lished, the plant was already widely grown in cottage gardens and was also known as Sweet Johns. Commenting on the plants' virtues, Gerard notes that "these plants are not used either in meat or medicine, but esteemed for their beauty to decke up gardens, the bosomes of the beautifull, garlands and crowns for pleasure." Clearly, Gerard was on the right track!

The historical event that certainly sealed the plants' name forever as Sweet William was the Battle of Culloden in 1745. It was here that the last remnants of the Scottish Jacobite forces who supported the right of James II and his descendants to the English throne were defeated by William, Duke of Cumberland, the overweight third son of King George II. When he returned to London in 1746 for the Georgian equivalent of a ticker-tape parade, the streets were strewn with petals, many of them those of Sweet William, and the name has stuck. I hope that it pleased William, temporarily at least, because when the details of the battle became better known, he entered the history books as "Bloody Butcher" and "Butcher Cumberland" for the atroc-

NAME: Sweet William *Dianthus barbatus*
HEIGHT: To 2' (60 cm)
EXPOSURE: Sun to part shade
BLOOMING PERIOD: Late spring, early summer
SOIL: Ordinary garden soil
COMPANIONS: Especially effective when planted around larger perennials that will begin to bloom as the Sweet William fades
SPECIAL NOTES: Old stock should be removed after two to three years, and be replaced with new plants

ities he committed on the battlefield. In a sort of botanical retaliation, the Scots named one of their most repugnant, evil-smelling plants (common ragwort) "Stinking Billy."

Sweet William first reached the shores of North America in the last half of the eighteenth century and has since naturalized across much of the eastern seaboard. Fortunately in those days plants didn't need passports or phyto-sanitary certificates.

∾ Sweet William Cultivars to Look Out For

'Auricula-Eyed' – An ancient strain, almost lost but recently resurrected, with each flower possessing an eye (a dark band around the center of the bloom). Fragrant; height to 18" (45 cm)

'Dunnett's Dark Crimson' – Introduced about 1930. Deep bronzy foliage with blood-red flowers; height to 24" (60 cm)

'Electron Strain' – A wide variety of red, pink and white bicolors with distinctive markings. Good for cutting; height to 24" (60 cm)

'Excelsior' – Mixed colors on double flowers, some bicolors. Height to 18" (45 cm).

'Super Duplex' – Almost 100 percent double flowers reselected from an old double strain; height to 15" (37 cm)

'Roundabout Series' – A dwarf, bushy variety, may be grown as annuals; height to 8" (20 cm)

'Wee Willie' – Very dwarf in shades of crimson, pink and white; height to 5" (12.5 cm)

Perennials

PERENNIALS REPRESENT LONG-TERM investments in the cottage garden, and careful forethought is essential when planning which ones to buy and how to place them. Many perennials can, of course, be started from seed, and this was the approach I took when I was an impecunious university student. However, in addition to taking about three years to flower, many perennial cultivars don't "come true" from seed — that is, they resemble one or other of their parents in subsequent generations. If this occurs, you may end up with small flowers instead of large ones, or they may be the wrong color, or the plants may be tall instead of short.

Specific cultivated varieties must instead be propagated vegetatively, sometimes by root division, sometimes by root or stem cuttings, and increasingly frequently by micropropagation. Micropropagation is the process whereby tiny fragments of a plant's growing tips are propagated in a laboratory, resulting in hundreds of plants, all of which are genetically identical. However, this process can be expensive and the costs are often passed on to the consumer. It therefore makes sense to learn about the specific conditions that individual species require in order to thrive, and to ensure that you can provide them before reaching for your credit card.

Although many perennials may require dividing after four or five years to keep them vigorous, you don't get many opportunities to amend the soil around (and underneath!) these static floral stands. With a scenario like this one, it's more important than ever to amend the soil well with plenty of compost, composted manure, or whatever material you normally use, in order to increase nutrient and organic matter levels within the soil profile. Later additions of these materials as a top dressing are helpful, but they can never replace a really good initial boost prior to plant installation.

When you're considering the placement of perennials, remember that there's more to it than the eventual height and width of the plant, and whether it prefers sun or shade, wet or dry. There is, of course, the color of the flowers — but it's almost impossible to clash in a cottage garden! What you must pay more attention to is leaf texture, shape and color. Perennials, after all, bloom for only a few weeks each year, which is why we supplement them with bulbs, annuals, biennials and vegetables. These plants make up for the stingier bloom periods of perennials, but gardeners are still left staring at a lot of foliage for most of the year.

Generally speaking, it's best to mix leaf types up as much as possible. If you have a grassy-leaved daylily, don't plant Siberian iris next to it! Rather, break up the monotony with the gaudy foliage of vegetable amaranth (*Amaranthus tricolor*), and throw in a lacy artemisia for added contrast. Perhaps you'll decide it prudent to tone the scene down with the dark leaves of white snakeroot (*Eupatorium rugosum* 'Chocolate'). Often the best of these combinations will happen by accident, so don't be reticent to try a mélange or two of your own devising.

Japanese anemone

Anemone x hybrida

UNLIKE SO MANY of the plants we've been discussing, Japanese anemones don't have a long history of cultivation in Western gardens. In fact, Japanese anemones, per se, are really a man-made creation, the result of crossing two Chinese species at the Royal Horticultural Society's garden at Chiswick during the mid-nineteenth century. While the species are in themselves beautiful plants, this is one clear case of further hybridizing actually improving a plant, rather than destroying it as is the case with so many plants that are stately and regal in the wild, but that look like crudely painted buffoons after the geneticists get their hands on them.

A member of the buttercup family (Ranunculaceae), the anemone genus comprises about 120 species, many of which will be familiar to gardeners. Most cottage gardens have a couple of patches of early spring windflowers (*A. blanda*), or poppy anemones (*A. coronaria*), and the British wood anemone (*A. nemorosa*) is becoming increasingly popular in North American shade and woodland gardens. There are even a few native species worthy of space in North American cottage gardens, such as the meadow anemone (*A. canadensis*), which bears pristine, starry white flowers in early summer. Native from Labrador to Colorado, this anemone requires moist soil in full sun and is hardy to zone 3. The even hardier *A. multifida* (zone 2) bears creamy yellow flowers in summer and grows about 12 inches (30 centimeters) tall.

The joy of Japanese anemones, apart from their unquestionably patrician form, is the time of year

Although a "man-made creation," fall-blooming Japanese anemones are without a doubt the crowning glory of the autumn garden. Gardeners in northern areas who think they can't grow good autumn-flowering anemones should look for the grape-leaved anemone (A. tomentosa, syn. A. vitifolia 'Robustissima') which, with a little mulching, is hardy to zones 4 to 5.

at which they flower. By mid-September, most of the other "important" perennials are past their prime, and those that are left tend to display the predominantly golden hues of autumn, so I'm always grateful to get some good pinks and whites back into the tapestry so late in the season.

When selecting autumn anemones, it's important to understand a bit about the parentage of the cultivars that are available and how they relate to each other. All true Japanese anemones are the result of crosses between *A. hupehensis* var. *japonica* and *A. vitifolia*. *A. vitifolia* was first discovered in 1827 by the wife of India's governor general, Lord Amherst. During a ten-month stay in the then un-Europeanized Simla (later to become the Raj's summer capital), Lady Amherst sent seeds of *A. vitifolia* and *Clematis montana* back to Britain. As an aside, the widely grown anemone 'Robustissima' is often sold as an *A. vitifolia* cultivar, but in fact it belongs to a separate species, *A. tomentosa*, which blooms slightly earlier.

The other parent of Japanese anemones is *A. hupehensis* var. *japonica*. Not really Japanese at all, this plant came to Britain via the efforts of Scottish plant hunter Robert Fortune (1812–90), who collected it on the ramparts of Shanghai among the graves. Many of the resulting cultivars of this subspecies are considered Japanese anemones, although technically, of course, they are not.

Now that the parental units are assembled, we can move on to the true Japanese anemones, the result of Chinese plants hybridized in Britain. Even botany has its ironic side! Japanese anemones are generally hardy to zones 4 or 5 and demand rich, fertile soil in part shade to full sun. In warmer zones these plants can become invasive, but they're so lovely that gardeners are usually hesitant to disturb thriving clumps. In the more frigid limits of their range, anemones may benefit from a protective mulch and rarely become overgrown. Although they

---

∾ *Anemone hupehensis* var. *japonica* Cultivars

'Bressingham Glow' — Very similar to 'Prinz Heinrich' and introduced by Alan Bloom

'Prinz Heinrich' ('Prince Henry') — Raised in Germany by Wilhelm Pfitzer in 1902. Very similar to the species, so much so that Graham Stuart Thomas comments, "It now appears they may be one and the same thing." Also offered occasionally as *A.* 'Profusion'

'Rosenschale' ('Pink Shell') — Dark rose-pink blooms

'September Charm' — Probably the best known of the group, 'September Charm' is sometimes thought to be a cultivar of the species *A. hupehensis*, rather than of the subspecies, var. *japonica*. Bearing pale pink flowers over a long period, this cultivar was introduced in 1932 by Bristol Nurseries. Another named variety thought to be a cultivar of the original *A. hupehensis* species is called 'Hadspen Abundance'. Raised by Eric Smith of *The Plantsman* fame, it bears purplish-pink flowers.

NAME: Japanese anemone *Anemone* x *hybrida*

HEIGHT: 3 to 4' (90 to 120 cm)

EXPOSURE: Part sun to shade

BLOOMING PERIOD: Late summer to late autumn

SOIL: Rich garden soil

COMPANIONS: Best grouped with plants that bloom about the same time such as yellow wax bells (*Kirengeshoma palmata*) or plants with bold foliage such as *Rodgersia* spp.

SPECIAL NOTES: Be careful when weeding in the spring not to uproot young anemone seedlings.

grow from 3 to 5 feet (90 to 150 cm) high, they seldom require staking. Japanese anemones range in color from pure white to deep pink; semi-double forms are available. Most Japanese anemones are sterile, so propagation (except for breeding purposes) is ordinarily by division.

Deadheading after the first flush of flowers have finished may encourage new flowering spikes, especially in warmer areas. Where most gardeners run into difficulty with Japanese anemones is early in the season. These plants are "late starters," often not showing any signs of life until early summer. I always leave my plant markers in the ground so I remember where they're located before their foliage appears — it's heartbreaking to uproot the crown of an $8 anemone to install a 25-cent Browallia bluebell!

Although Japanese anemones don't have a long pedigree in British cottage gardens, nor can we sneak them in the back door as native species, our North American cottage gardens would be immeasurably poorer without them. When they were first bred in Britain, anemones were grown strictly under glass as they were thought to be too tender and rare to endure the vagaries of British weather. Clearly, they've come a long way since then.

❧ Japanese Anemone (*A. x hybrida*) Cultivars

'Geante des Blanches' ('White Queen') – Derived from an Irish seedling of 'Honorine Jobert' re-named 'Lady Ardilaun', the French company Lemoine introduced this third generation anemone prior to World War I.

'Honorine Jobert' – The great-grandmother of most of the modern cultivars, this classic, single white-flowered form was introduced in 1858. Gorgeous.

'Konigin Charlotte' ('Queen Charlotte') – Introduced by Pfitzer (Germany) in 1898, this cultivar is often considered the best large-flowered variety, bearing sumptuous mid-pink blooms.

'Luise Uhink' – Also introduced by Pfitzer in 1898, this still popular cultivar has large white blooms with up to ten sepals. (Like four o'clocks, the blooming parts of these plants are actually sepals, not petals.)

'Pamina' – Probably the darkest anemone with double rose-red flowers.

'Whirlwind' – A U.S. introduction from 1887, this is one of my favorites. The last of the anemones to bloom with blowsy, semi-double white flowers. Purists will shun you!

Black snakeroot

Cimicifuga simplex

BLACK SNAKEROOT (or autumn cohosh) is the last of the herbaceous plants to bloom in most cottage gardens, and where winter comes unexpectedly early, the frosts may nip the blooms before you get a chance to. Hardy to zones 3 to 4, black snakeroot grows between 3 and 4 feet (90 to 120 cm) high, and the pure white blooms have been described as looking like elaborately constructed bottle brushes on arching wands. The handsome foliage is deeply divided and segmented with numerous leaflets and may be bright green or brownish purple. Black snakeroot requires deep fertile soil with plenty of organic matter, and once planted, clumps should be left undisturbed. *Cimicifuga* grows naturally in part sun to almost full shade, but avoid planting it near tree roots as it will resent the competition for moisture and nutrients. One of the best attributes of

At Raven Hill Herb Farm on Vancouver Island, Cimicifuga simplex *'Atropurpurea' struts its stuff across the autumn landscape. Because it resents disturbance from indecisive gardeners or competition from tree roots, choose your planting site carefully, add organic matter, and then leave it alone except to make sure it has sufficient moisture during its first year, thereby enabling the plant to establish a healthy root system.*

Cimicifuga is that it never needs staking, a virtue all too rare among tall plants.

Cimicifuga is another member of the multi-talented Ranunculaceae or buttercup family, and there are about 20 species of *Cimicifuga* fairly evenly distributed across the northern hemisphere. When gardeners pick up black snakeroot cultivars at their local nursery, they may think that they're buying a native species, but in fact, they probably aren't.

Only two native species of *Cimicifuga* might be found in gardens, and they are the medicinally active black cohosh (*C. racemosa*), which is gaining a reputation as a natural remedy for menstrual complaints, menopause and arthritis; and *C. rubifolia* (formerly known as *C. racemosa* var. *cordifolia*). Certainly both plants are worthy of space in your garden, but neither has any named cultivars, and both bloom somewhat earlier than *C. simplex*. As if this wasn't perplexing enough, many texts and plant tags may still erroneously refer to yet another species, *C. ramosa*. Botanical taxonomists have, in their wisdom, decided that there is no such thing, and any plant that might have been referred to as *C. ramosa* in the past is now considered just another form of *C. simplex*. Simple!

The cimicifugas are seasoned travelers, and while samples of our North American black cohosh (*C. racemosa*) were dutifully sent to the Chelsea Physic Garden as early as 1732, it wasn't until 1879 that *C. simplex* made it from Japan to the West. *C. simplex* is also sometimes called Kamchatka bugbane due to its natural distribution: it grows in a straight line up through Japan, then northwards to the Russian Sakhalin and Kuril Islands, and finally to the Kamchatka Peninsula, just across the water from Alaska. So it's *almost* native. The common name of snakeroot refers to its antiquated use as a remedy for snakebites, while *cohosh* is Algonquin for "it is rough," presumably referring to the texture of the roots.

No doubt the reason that *C. simplex* is prized above other members of the genus is related in part to its flowering so late in the season, almost thumbing its nose at the imminent approach of winter. A highly ornamental plant to begin with, this is the species that hybridizers have concentrated on, and there are some wonderful cultivars available. Black snakeroot is not the easiest plant to grow from seed, needing as it does alternate cold and warm periods in order to initiate germination, a process known as stratification. Seedlings from mature plants are scanty, and individual cultivars will not always come true from seed, although some seed strains (e.g., 'Brunette' and 'Atropurpurea') are available. Instead, black snakeroot is usually propagated commercially by root division or rooted cuttings, and therefore they aren't the most inexpensive specimens you'll ever buy, but they're worth every penny.

NAME: Black snakeroot *Cimicifuga simplex*

HEIGHT: 3 to 4' (90 to 120 cm)

EXPOSURE: Shade

BLOOMING PERIOD: Autumn

SOIL: Rich, with plenty of organic matter

COMPANIONS: *Houttuynia cordata* 'Chameleon' leaves provide a dramatic contrast to the ferny foliage of black snakeroot, or a planting of wintergreen (*Gaultheria procumbens*) will cover its bare ankles

SPECIAL NOTES: Most members of the *Cimicifuga* genus have at one time or another been included in the closely related *Actaea* (or Baneberry) clan. Recently, botanists have decided to move all species of *Cimicifuga* back into *Actaea*, which is how we should correctly refer to them in the future. Because the change is so recent I have retained the name *Cimicifuga* to avoid confusion during the period of transition.

⮞ Black Snakeroot (*Cimicifuga simplex*) Cultivars

'Atropurpurea' – Purplish leaves and buds, considered an improvement on 'Braunlaub'

'Braunlaub' – An older German cultivar with brown leaves, the forerunner of 'Atropurpurea' and 'Brunette'

'Brunette' – With even darker leaves (a rich purplish black) than 'Atropurpurea', it's important to protect the foliage from strong afternoon sun to avoid fading. Introduced by Blooms from Denmark, this is a "brag plant," with a price tag to match.

'Elstead variety' – An older British cultivar, purple buds open to expose pure white flowers very late in the season.

Graham Stuart Thomas calls this "a plant of exceeding grace and a great treasure."

'Hillside Black Beauty' and 'Black Negligee' – The most recent *C. simplex* cultivars, and even more expensive than 'Brunette', with leaves that are supposedly darker, although I find it difficult to distinguish between them. Time will tell.

'White Pearl' ('Armleuchter') – The oldest cultivar still in commerce, 'White Pearl' was introduced in 1923. With mid-green foliage, and at a fraction of the price of newer cultivars, four 'White Pearl' framing a single 'Brunette' or 'Black Negligee' will make a dramatic statement without leaving you bankrupt.

Delphinium

Delphinium hybrids

MOST GARDENERS WILL consider that delphiniums are essential components of the cottage garden style, preferably coupled with some pink antique roses. This view is valid to a degree, but delphiniums are anything but "traditional" cottage garden plants. Like Japanese anemones, the delphiniums we know today are strictly man-made creations, and before the middle of the nineteenth century, they simply didn't exist. No doubt the native English delphinium or annual larkspur (*Consolida ajacis*), a favorite of both the Tudor and Stuart monarchs, was grown in cottage gardens, but delphiniums "proper" were not.

Ironically, the delphinium was not at first singled out for its beautiful flowering spikes, but for its seed, as an antidote to scorpion bites. It was the Roman Emperor Nero's Greek physician Dioscorides who first suggested this treatment in his *Materia Medica*, a list of herbs considered useful in medicine. About the same time, the name *Delphinium* (from the Greek word for "small dolphin") was attached to the plant, because the shape of its unopened buds looked similar to a dolphin in profile.

Essentially a plant of mountainous regions, delphiniums are scattered across the globe, with the exception of Australia and the two poles. Several species are native to the Rockies, and these plants will thrive when they are grown in the areas to which they are indigenous. If you can provide the ideal conditions, keep an eye out for *D. cardinale*, *D. nudicaule* and *D. trolliifolium*, all native to western North America. It's the perfect plant for high altitudes, and I well remember banks of delphinium, both wild species (*D. cashmerianum*) and garden escapees, blanketing the hillsides around Srinagar, Kashmir (6,000 feet/1,800 meters) when I was a child. Indeed, healthy five-foot (1.5 meter) spikes have been observed at almost twice that altitude in Leadville, Colorado, at 10,150 feet (3,000 meters). Evidently, delphiniums like a view!

The majority of delphiniums that we grow today are known as the Elatum Group, which is rather misleading. Seeds of the pale blue-flowered species *D. elatum* (widely distributed across Eurasia) were first introduced into cultivation at St. Petersburg about 1597. A century and a half later, a French horticulturist offered seeds of *D. elatum* for sale to the general public. Soon, other species of delphinium (notably *D. grandiflorum*, still available as the cultivar 'Blue Butterfly' or 'Blue Elf') were grown together with *D. elatum*. Before long, unassisted by anything but the bees, these species began to cross-pollinate with one another, producing an improved race of plants. The hybridized seed was then collected from the *D. elatum* parent plants, due to their prolific seed-bearing capabilities. Since then, the name 'Elatum' has stuck, although this species represents only part of the genetic material present in most modern cultivars.

It wasn't until 1848 that French nurseryman Victor Lemoine began to improve the existing delphinium strains by deliberate cross-pollination, raising hundreds of hybrids every year and selecting only the best. By 1880, Lemoine's crosses were receiving considerable attention and acclaim, and it was at this point that Englishman James Kelway imported some of Lemoine's progeny to his Somerset nursery. Over the course of the next 40 years, Kelway introduced many new cultivars, widening the color range and improving the form of the plants as he went.

Probably the most important event to influence the advent of our modern delphiniums was the partnership between gardener Charles Langdon and innkeeper James Blackmore, together forming the firm of Blackmore and Langdon in 1901. By 1907, Blackmore and Langdon were offering their own delphinium cultivars for sale, hybridized by using the existing plants that had been developed by Lemoine and Kelway. After a brief interruption during World War I, the firm started up again and produced up to 100,000 seedlings every year. In the ten years between 1925 and 1935, Blackmore and Langdon won 45 out of a possible 96 Royal Horticultural Society (RHS) Delphinium Trial Awards, basically blowing the other 107 or so competitors out of the water. Reaching their peak in the period between the wars, Blackmore and Langdon were responsible not only for developing improved strains of delphinium, but also for popularizing them. Unhappily, their breeding program ended in 1978, but fortunately the Society began breeding delphiniums at their Wisley garden in 1980, much of the work concentrating on developing a hardy red-flowered plant.

In the midst of this European flurry of activity, a Czech named Frank Reinelt emigrated to California in 1925 and set about creating a new strain of delphinium, partly to increase the range of colors available, but principally for the production of seed, for both the American and European markets. Little attention was paid to maintaining the delphinium's semi-perennial habit, and as a result, many of Reinelt's plants began to behave more like annuals than perennials. His strain became known as 'Pacific Giants', and they are with us still, accounting for the majority of delphiniums currently established in North American gardens.

A gorgeous display of 'Pacific Giant' delphiniums, the legacy of Czech breeder Frank Reinelt, who worked on developing new delphinium strains encompassing a wider color range in California during the 1920s. Although prone to disease, the majority of delphiniums currently being grown in North America belong to the 'Pacific Giant' series, and it's certainly hard to argue with blooms like these, even if the plants are short-lived!

While the form of its plants and color range expanded, the delphinium's tolerance to insects and disease diminished. This is unfortunate, but unavoidable. The one thing that North American gardeners absolutely must do is adjust their expectations. Delphinium cultivars should never be considered anything more or less than short-lived perennials. The average life expectancy is about three years, and if you succeed in getting four years out of a plant, you're doing well.

No one would ever accuse delphiniums of being low-maintenance, but considering the floral display that a single plant can achieve at maturity, it's worth a little extra work. Staking is my least favorite job in the garden — in fact, I hate it. If a plant requires seasonal staking, I won't grow it, unless it's a delphinium. Strong, thin stakes should be placed around plants in the spring, when foliage is about 8 inches (20 centimeters) high.

Delphiniums don't deserve their reputation as difficult plants — just don't expect them to outlive your peonies. Insects can be sprayed with insecticidal soap, and in the case of serious disease, plants should be removed and burned (never compost diseased plant material). I usually get some black leaf spot (*Psuedomonas delphinii*) on my plants about midsummer, but providing the affected leaves are removed promptly, the problem never becomes serious. Many diseases can be avoided by thinning plants early in the season to avoid excessive congestion and improve air circulation around the crown.

Many gardeners like to remove the side shoots from flowering spikes. The idea is that the main spike (or leader) will grow larger, although I'm not convinced of that. Certainly, with this method, the plants will look tidier while in bloom. Once flowering has finished, many gardeners cut back the flowering spikes to the first leaf, thinking that the plant must maintain its foliage to nourish the roots for the following year. This is a sound idea for most perennials, but not so smart for delphiniums. In the first place, they aren't going to last forever anyway, so worrying about nutrient levels for the next decade or so is time wasted.

The best approach for North American cottage gardeners is to cut the plants right down to their crowns after flowering, and the reason is twofold. In the first place, this is the best way to encourage a second flush of bloom, and what gardener wouldn't aim for that? After shearing, give the plant a good drink with some high-phosphorus water-soluble fertilizer (no slow-release soil conditioners for this procedure), and within a week or two you will be rewarded with lovely, fresh growth and possibly several flower spikes. The other benefit of treating the plants in this manner is that it tends to disrupt disease and insect cycles, reducing the need for sprays, organic or otherwise. Mrs. C. W. Earle, author of *Pot-pourri from a Surrey Garden* (1897), puts it well when she says, "They may be cut down bravely after flowering; it does them no harm, and they often break again and have stray flowering sprays in the autumn." So be brave!

In addition to the Elatum hybrids, there is one other that deserves mention, and that is the 'Connecticut Yankee' strain. Slightly shorter at 2 feet (60 centimeters), these plants don't require staking, and although they are even less long-lived than the Elatum hybrids, they perform better than other varieties in the Midwest.

Since individual delphinium plants have a limited life expectancy in any North American garden, I buy a couple of 3.5-inch (9 centimeter) pots (seedlings) every year to replenish plants that may have perished over the winter. Their demise will be due to age, rather than to lack of hardiness — most delphiniums are hardy to zones 2 to 3. These young plants are inexpensive and take much less time and effort than raising your own progeny from seed, and you can also take advantage of the new color combinations that seem to appear every year.

Every plant needs a prima donna in the group, and the new forms of "red" delphinium absolutely fill the bill. I'm not sure yet how I feel about a red delphinium. My favorite combos consist of pure white, light blue and blue-black, all grown together, and the 'Round Table' series (e.g., 'Black Knight', 'Galahad', 'Guinevere' and 'King Arthur') achieves this aim admirably. Nevertheless, 'Red Rocket' has already hit the sales floor, the result of intense breeding (using California natives *D. cardinale* and *D. nudicaule*) and tissue culture (micropropagation).

The jury is still out on these new red cultivars, and they are very expensive. While I'm not averse to shelling out big money for a tree peony that will very likely outlive me, I'm not so sure about spending the same amount on a plant that may last only two

or three years. I'm tempted though: surely a red delphinium would look arresting placed next to a primrose-yellow type like 'Sunbeam'? Or would I be drummed out of the English Cottage Garden Society?

Lupine

Lupinus hybrids

I SUSPECT THAT like so many of my generation, I first became cognizant of lupines via the Monty Python "Dennis Moore" sketch. Dennis Moore was a Robin Hood wannabe. However, he got it wrong somewhere along the way, and instead of bringing the poor money and jewels, he brought them lupines. As silly as this may sound, we must remember that the members of Monty Python were all astoundingly well educated, and this skit was, to a degree, based on fact. The European white lupine (*L. albus*) was grown as cattle fodder in days gone by, and during times of great hardship, humans ate them as well, so it's far from inconceivable that the medieval poor were reduced to an occasional main course of Lupine Chow.

The lupine genera contains about 200 species, a few native to the Mediterranean region, but the vast majority native to the Americas. The name lupine is derived from the Latin *lupus*, meaning "wolf." In ancient times it was believed that lupines robbed the soil of nutrients in the same way that wolves robbed shepherds of their sheep. It's a member of the pea family (*Leguminosae*), so the exact opposite is true; lupines, like all members of the pea family, are

NAME: ✻Delphinium (some) *Delphinium* spp. and hybrids

HEIGHT: To 6' (1.8 m)

EXPOSURE: Sun

BLOOMING PERIOD: Summer

SOIL: Rich garden soil

COMPANIONS: Great with tall lilies (*Lilium* spp. and cultivars) and can be effectively under-planted with ✻grass nut (*Triteleia laxa* 'Koningin Fabiola' — formerly classified as *Brodiaea*)

SPECIAL NOTES: Keep an eye out for native species of *Delphinium* indigenous to your area

Nowhere but in North America could you hope to see such an outstanding display of our native blue lupine (L. polyphyllus). It's happiest on the east and west coasts of the continent, so inland gardeners must be contented to commence their initiation with the 'Band of Nobles' series, many of which will bloom the first year from seed, often continuing well into the autumn.

capable of fixing atmospheric nitrogen in their roots, actually enriching the soil.

Although most of us think of lupines as being as much a part of the calendar image of the cottage garden as is a small blond child in a pinafore, lupines, like the delphinium, are relatively recent introductions. It wasn't until 1826 that Scottish plant collector David Douglas (1799–1834) gathered seeds of *L. polyphyllus* near Vancouver, British Columbia, and sent them back to the Horticultural Society of London. Most of our modern "border lupines" are largely derived from this sun-loving native plant.

For almost 100 years, the lupine was principally grown by amateurs who traded seed with one another, helping to increase the spread of garden varieties. During this early period of lupine cultivation, it wasn't unusual for gardeners to maintain their own seed strains, and this is what Gertrude Jekyll did at her garden at Munstead Wood, selecting and re-selecting only those plants that exhibited the colors she admired. She grew pinks, blues and pale purples, as well as a lovely pure white variety that eventually became known as 'Munstead White'.

Finally in 1911, in the true spirit of cottage gardening, a gardener named George Russell began selecting and crossing lupines at his allotment garden in York, England. In addition to using *L. polyphyllus*, he also used the tree lupine (*L. arboreus*) from California and the annual *L. hartwegii* from Mexico to widen the range of colors he was able to produce. He quietly worked away at his task for over a quarter of a century until, in 1937, his lupines suddenly attracted attention, and he won the coveted RHS Gold Medal. The result of Russell's work culminated in the launching of the 'Russell Hybrids', a strain that dominated garden lupines for the next 60 years.

Sadly, in recent years, a seed-borne disease has attacked most strains of 'Russell' lupines, gradually infecting and then killing young seedlings. As a result, most nurseries have been unsuccessful in propagating these plants, and they have all but disappeared. Some experts suggest that this problem is magnified in greenhouse operations, and that seeds of the 'Russell' strain stand a much better chance of survival if planted directly out in the open garden in spring. On a happier note, much of Russell's original work has been resurrected by the Woodfield Brothers in England, who are now producing some very fine new cultivars.

Hybrid lupines require reasonably moist soil in full to part sun if they are to prosper. They should not be grown in freshly manured ground — in fact, it

ꙮ Lupines Anyone?

Like *Cannabis sativa* (marijuana), lupines have been considered at various times as plants with an infinite number of applications. Mrs. Grieve gives an amusing account of a dinner held to celebrate the diverse possibilities of the white lupine.

In 1917 a 'Lupin' banquet was given in Hamburg at a botanical gathering, at which a German Professor, Dr. Thoms, described the multifarious uses to which the lupin might be put. At a table covered with a tablecloth of lupin fibre, lupin soup was served; after the soup came lupin beefsteak, roasted in lupin oil and seasoned with lupin extract, then bread containing 20 percent of lupin, lupin margerine and cheese of lupin albumen, and finally lupin liqueur and lupin coffee. Lupin soap served for washing the hands, while lupin-fibre paper and envelopes with lupin adhesive were available for writing.

Dennis Moore (and John Cleese) would have loved it!

would be wasted on them. They prefer soil that is on the lean side, with a pH near neutral. Many garden texts suggest a slightly acid soil, but this is pertinent only if you're growing a lupine species, rather than a garden cultivar. If your lupines are destined for a vase, be sure to fill their hollow stems with water (hold them upside down under running water to fill the stems) before placing them in the container, as this will extend their vase life greatly.

Lupines should be considered short-lived perennials, although I have some plants over ten years old. Fortunately, they're very easy to start from seed, and I don't think I've ever actually purchased a plant. Seeds should be started in a sterile soilless mix indoors several weeks before the last frost date, or they can be directly seeded in the garden. Once you have a decent stand of lupines established, all that is needed is four to six seedlings every year to replace the plants lost over the winter.

Lupine hybrids are generally hardy to zones 3 to 4, although it appears that yellow-flowered varieties are slightly less hardy than other types, perhaps because the genes producing yellow flowers are predominantly derived from Californian and Mexican species.

Lupines are available in dwarf cultivars seldom reaching 2 feet (60 centimeters) tall, as well as others that normally attain heights of 5 feet (1.5 meters). If you grow the very tall varieties, some staking may be required if they are grown in an exposed situation. Should lupines be allowed to go to seed, they may behave more like biennials than perennials. On the other hand, if they are cut down to their crowns after blooming, fresh foliage will appear, and you may be rewarded with a second flush of bloom. I sometimes compromise between the two extremes, and trim plants back by half, leaving a seedpod or two to mature for some low-

❧ *Lupinus* Cultivars for the Cottage Garden

'Band of Nobles' series – A wonderful strain containing all the colors: white, yellow, pink, red, blue and lots of bicolors, usually with white or yellow in combination with another color. Many plants will bloom the first year from seed, and mature plants can reach a height of 5' (1.5 m).

'Gallery Hybrids' – A dwarf variety (height 16 to 20"/40 to 50 cm) available in either individual colors or as a mixture. Disciplined and well-behaved in the border.

'Lulu' mix – Hate the name, but this is a worthy British strain, available in a good range of colors and bicolors. 'Lulu' possesses a more pronounced perennial habit than many lupines, especially the dusty rose-colored types; height to 30" (75 cm)

L. hartwegii ssp. *cruckshankii* 'Sunrise' – A fragrant annual lupine from Mexico that is in dire need of a common name. In spring, seeds should be sown directly in the open ground. Blue, white, bronze and gold, all on one plant; height to 30" (75 cm). Visitors will stop dead in their tracks!

'Russell Hybrids' – The beleaguered original strain of 1937. Where seed is still available, it should be sown *in situ*.

Woodfield Brothers cultivars – These plants have taken up where the 'Russell' strain left off. Many individual cultivars are now available, both in solids and bicolors. Usually sold as mature plants, seed strains should also come true to type, height to 36" (90 cm). Look for 'Catherine of York', 'Chandelier', 'The Chatelaine', 'Magnificence', 'My Castle', 'Noble Maiden', 'The Governor', 'The Page' and other equally heraldic epithets.

maintenance propagation. Many hybrid varieties will also assume a biennial habit when grown at high altitudes. Slugs and aphids are troublesome occasionally, but no more so on lupines than most other plants in the cottage garden.

NAME: Lupine *Lupinus* spp. and hybrids

HEIGHT: To 4' (120 cm)

EXPOSURE: Sun to part sun

BLOOMING PERIOD: Summer

SOIL: Ordinary garden soil

COMPANIONS: Look for plants that provide interest and contrast such as evening primrose (*Oenothera triloba*) and variegated comfrey (*Symphytum* 'Goldsmith')

SPECIAL NOTES: Leave one or two of the bottom seed pods on the plant to ripen, thereby ensuring seedlings for the following year

Penstemon

Penstemon spp. and hybrids

THERE'S NO DOUBT that there's a penstemon for every cottage garden, and for every cottage gardener. With no fewer than 250 species and at least the same number of cultivars, there are certainly plenty to choose from. Some will be at home in the mountains or subalpine regions, while others will prefer the extremes of a prairie climate. Members of the snapdragon family (Scrophulariaceae), penstemons are often considered the North American equivalent of their near relation, the foxglove (*Digitalis* spp.), despite the penstemons' constituting a far more diverse group.

The majority of the genus tend to occur on the western side of the continent, but the first "documented" discovery of penstemons took place in the East, despite the fact that native Americans had long used the plant to relieve toothache. In 1748 a Virginia doctor named John Mitchell (1711–68) described *P. laevigatus*, closely related to the more widely known *P. digitalis*. He communicated his findings to Linnaeus (the patriarch of modern botanical nomenclature), and although their correspondence was genial, Linnaeus decided that the plant was just a new species of *Chelone* (or turtlehead), another North American native with which he was already familiar.

Mitchell had already coined the name "penstemon," which alluded to the unusual fifth stamen (from the Greek *pente*, meaning "five"). In the end, Linnaeus compromised and called the plant *Chelone pentstemon*, altering the spelling slightly to be sure that the meaning wouldn't escape anyone. It is only recently that the penstemons have been removed from the genus *Chelone* and been assigned one of their own.

Penstemons were slow to catch on in Europe, but by the middle of the nineteenth century, they were well known by specialists. European breeding (mostly in Britain and Germany) of the genus went on fitfully for the next hundred or so years, eventually producing a race of highly ornamental large-flowered hybrids. Unfortunately, these particular plants are hardy only to zone 7 or 8, and so not viable for many North American cottage gardeners. Nevertheless, if you live in a sufficiently temperate zone, give a try to some of these colonials that went to school in Europe.

Since there are so many penstemons to choose from, gardeners who live in areas where penstemon species are indigenous should introduce them into their borders. Seed for these plants is invariably available at local exchanges, or you could contact the American Penstemon Society in Lakewood, Colorado. You should also always be ready to exploit your own microclimate, since you may represent one of the very few gardeners able to successfully grow a particular species.

Luckily for gardeners like me, there is no dearth of penstemon species and cultivars that are hardy in some of North America's colder areas. The majority of penstemons will appreciate full to part sun, in reasonably good garden soil. Not particularly fussy plants, penstemons are occasionally prone to attack by common garden pests such as slugs and aphids, but such problems are rarely serious. Penstemon cultivars are usually purchased as plants at garden centers, but some are available as "seed strains" due to the increasing demand for the genus after *P. digitalis* 'Husker Red' was named American Perennial Plant of the Year in 1996. I've found that direct seeding is less successful than starting them indoors in seed trays, and only some cultivars will be reliably true to type.

Penstemons tend to be short-lived perennials, surviving on average for between three and six years. Preventing plants from setting seed will undoubtedly prolong the life of plants, and penstemons don't seed very readily in really cold zones anyway. If, after flowering, the foliage of a plant is still ornamental (as in 'Husker Red'), then only the spent flowering spike should be removed. If the foliage has deteriorated to the point of being unsightly (as is sometimes the case with *P. digitalis*), then all growth

should be cut back to the crown of the plant, where new basal rosettes of foliage will soon be formed. Secondary bloom may sometimes also be achieved using this method, although you may end up shortening the life of a plant as it "blooms itself to death." As with lupines, a few seedlings produced every spring by your own fair hands will make up for any winter casualties.

The first type of hardy penstemon we should look at is the beardlip penstemon, or *P. barbatus*. Native to western North America and hardy to zone 4, this was the first penstemon to be offered as seed to the British gardening public in 1835. As is so

> ## ❧ Penstemon Cultivars that are Hardy to Zone 7 or 8
>
> 'Alice Hindley' – (Introduced 1931, England) Large mauve flowers with white throats
>
> 'Garnet' – (Introduced 1918, Switzerland) The trade name in English-speaking countries for 'Andenken an Friedrich Hahn'. Crimson flowers and dark-colored stems.
>
> 'King George V' – (Introduced 1911, England) Royal scarlet with a white throat
>
> 'Mother of Pearl' – (Introduced 1984, England) Creamy white suffused with mauve, and throat heavily pencilled in darker mauve
>
> 'Purple Passion' – (Introduced 1989, New Zealand) Upright, deep purple flowers
>
> 'Scarlet Queen' – (Introduced 1932, Germany) The English trade name for 'Scharlachkoenigin'. Large-flowered red-and-white strain, easily propagated from seed.
>
> 'Sour Grapes' – (Introduced 1930s, England) Violet blue with a white throat and maroon markings
>
> 'Snowstorm' – (A synonym for 'White Bedder,' introduced 1912, England) Solid white flowers

Introduced in 1918, Penstemon *'Garnet' represents one of our native "tender" penstemons (zones 7 to 8) that went to finishing school in Switzerland. Cottage gardeners in colder zones will be thrilled with the cast-iron constitutions of the* P. barbatus *'Prairie' series, or of that other well-known Nebraskan,* P. digitalis *'Husker Red'.*

often the case, not much happened for a century, until in 1948, a floppy cultivar known as 'Flathead Lake' emerged. Although hardly prepossessing in and of itself, 'Flathead Lake' gave rise to an incredible number of cultivars and deserves to be remembered sympathetically by virtue of its progeny.

The first penstemons I ever grew from seed were *P. digitalis*, which had been purchased through a seed exchange at the University of Guelph, Ontario. Gathered from the wild at a donor's summer property near Peterborough, they sprouted readily and produced lovely compact plants in various shades of white, pink, mauve and purple. They survived for four years and perished, I am sure, because I allowed them to go to seed. Nevertheless, they made an exceptionally lovely addition to the borders, and I placed some of their turtlehead kin (*Chelone obliqua*) nearby. The flowers of both genera are similar, and the turtlehead began to take over nicely as the penstemons started to fade in mid-July.

Naturally occurring in fields and open woods from the Dakotas east to Quebec and Maine, *P. digitalis* is hardy to zone 2. The only well-known cultivar of this species is 'Husker Red', an introduction from Nevada's North Platte Research Center in the early 1980s. This cultivar was developed from a partly red-leaved plant found growing in the state and bears striking white flowers held well above the wine-red foliage. Strictly speaking, 'Husker Red' should only be propagated clonally, since seed strains usually produce inferior plants. The name of this cultivar is derived from the term "Corn Husker," slang for a local Nebraskan.

Another extremely useful form of penstemon is to be found in the evergreen sub-shrub *P. fruticosus* (or shrubby penstemon), native to several northern states, and to the hot interior of British Columbia in particular. Extremely drought tolerant, this species requires good drainage and is hardy to zone 4. It can be used to cascade over walls, or it looks great on a berm, growing as it does to only about 12 inches (30 centimeters) high, and covered with purple-blue flowers in early summer. In 1992, the University of British Columbia's Native Plant Program introduced the even more compact cultivar called 'Purple Haze'. An improvement over the species, 'Purple Haze' is covered with lilac-purple flowers in late spring and grows only 8 inches (20 centimeters) high. Hummingbirds love the tubular flowers, so be sure to include several penstemons in your North American cottage garden. They'll feel right at home.

Hardy *Penstemon barbatus* Cultivars

'Elfin Pink' – (USA, 1978) A dwarf variety, reaching just 12" (30 cm). Recommended for dry situations, and also available as a seed strain.

'Nanus Praecox' – Of uncertain origin, but clearly hybridized to be shorter and earlier-blooming than the species. Available as a seed strain in a variety of colors. Sometimes called 'Rondo'.

'Prairie' Series – Three very reliable cultivars have been released from the Horticultural Research Center of the University of Nebraska at North Platte. The first was 'Prairie Fire', a vigorous low-growing plant with scarlet flowers, registered in 1958. This was followed in 1969 by 'Prairie Dawn', with clear, light pink flowers. Finally, 'Prairie Dusk' was registered in 1990, producing flowers of a deep violet-purple.

NAME: ❦ Penstemon *Penstemon* spp. and hybrids
HEIGHT: 2 to 3' (60 to 90 cm)
EXPOSURE: Sun to part shade
BLOOMING PERIOD: Summer to early autumn
SOIL: Ordinary to rich garden soil
COMPANIONS: The closely related and later-blooming ❦ turtlehead (*Chelone* spp.) makes a natural companion as does the spring-blooming ❦ Canada columbine (*Aquilegia canadensis*)
SPECIAL NOTES: Deadhead regularly to encourage a perennial habit

Sea holly

 Eryngium spp. and cultivars

I CAN'T IMAGINE a cottage garden in high summer without at least one member of the *Eryngium* clan bursting forth through the blatant colors of its neighbors to reveal stately gray-blue flowers, looking like a majestic battleship sailing through a fireworks display. A sea holly in bloom is never dull. The stiff, metallic flowers are usually at the center of a cloud of frenzied beneficial insects, all waiting their turn for a sip of nectar. During the three or four weeks that eryngiums flower, they are always a hub of garden activity.

Most of the eryngiums grown in gardens are of European origin, although several native species as well as quite a few semitropical ones grow naturally from Mexico to South America. While the American species are quite distinct and represent a fairly straightforward group, the European ones are a tangled mess, and many plants that used to be considered separate species are now thought to be hybrids derived from a number of different species. It's probably not a very useful exercise for gardeners to try to sort out this labyrinth of loose ends. Suffice to say that such meritorious subjects as *Eryngium x oliverianum*, *E. x tripartitum*, and *E. x zabelii* are all of garden origin and of complicated ancestry.

Flat-leaf sea holly (*E. planum*) and its cultivars suffer from the same general confusion. Still classed as its own species, *E. planum* could well be the next candidate for a name change. As long ago as 1914, E. A. Bowles observed that "*E. planum*, and its many allied forms or aliases, whichever way you regard them, according to your character as a splitter or lumper, are tall effective plants . . ." I guess that makes me a "splitter," but whatever its origins, flat-leaf sea holly makes a lovely addition to the cottage garden. Compact cultivars of *E. planum*, usually reaching heights of only about 18 inches (45 centimeters), include 'Blaukappe', 'Blauer Zwerg' ('Blue Dwarf'), 'Blue Diamond', 'Blue Ribbon' and 'Silverstone'.

The *Eryngium* with the longest history of cultivation in cottage gardens is the maritime sea holly (*E. maritimum*). Native to the coastal areas of Britain and Europe, this salt-tolerant plant is also shorter than some of the others at about 24 inches (60 centimeters). Technically speaking it's a wildflower, and it's unlikely you'll find it at your garden center, but it is available from seed houses. Graham Stuart Thomas remarked that "it is strange that this beautiful native is not more often grown," and Gertrude Jekyll wrote of "the wild sea holly of our coasts, with leaves almost blue, and a handsome tuft of flower nearly matching them in colour."

All the European sea hollies are hardy to zone 4.

They prefer full sun and are happy in ordinary garden soil. They are pest-free plants and also quite drought tolerant, with a longer than average season of bloom. They may be cut for fresh flower bouquets or used in dried arrangements. If a few flower heads are allowed to set seed at the end of the summer, you will be rewarded with plenty of young plants the following spring. Although never invasive, one sea holly plant can spread to quite a substantial size after a few years. In spite of this, they never seem to take up too much room, their airy, statuesque form being extremely accommodating to nearby plants.

During the reign of Elizabeth I (1558–1603), sea holly root was candied and sold as a breath freshener or "kissing-comfit," and later the roots were eaten as sweets, known as "eringoes," which were apparently available until the 1860s.

The Elizabethans and the Jacobeans were both enthusiastic about sea holly, possibly because they were aware of its supposed aphrodisiac qualities, a reputation it had acquired as far back as Saxon times. In his *Herball* of 1597, Gerard recommended that eringoes should be administered to the elderly, saying, "They are exceedingly good to be given to old and aged people that are consumed and withered with age, and who want natural moisture." Gerard also adds that they are useful "to secure a stray lover," yet another practical attribute!

The first *Eryngium* that I ever grew (from seed, and quite effortlessly) was alpine sea holly (*E. alpinum*), and it was a good place to start. Probably the easiest and most ornamental of the sea hollies, this plant reaches a height of 30 inches (75 centimeters) at maturity and bears some of the largest flowers of the genus. Our old friend William Robinson writes in *The English Flower Garden* (1883), "When well grown [it] is not surpassed in beauty by any plant" — high praise

I consider the tale of how Miss Willmott's Ghost (Eryngium giganteum) acquired its name one of the most engaging of horticultural yarns. Like all the sea hollies, E. giganteum attracts a plethora of beneficial insects to the cottage garden, and who's to say that one day you won't engage in a spot of guerilla gardening yourself?

indeed! Native to the Alps from France to the former Yugoslavia, alpine sea holly usually makes its home in subalpine meadows (5,000 to 6,000 feet/1,500 to 1,800 meters) on limey soils, but it will tolerate slightly acidic conditions.

A few cultivars of alpine sea holly are available. 'Amethyst' (not to be confused with the separate species *E. amethystinum*) has smaller (1-inch/2.5 centimeter) flowerheads in a rich violet-blue color. A second cultivar called 'Donardt's Blue' is sometimes available, but I'm not convinced that this isn't actually a misnomer for the 'Donard Variety' strain introduced in 1913, and technically a further cultivar of *E. xzabelii* (to begin splitting hairs again!). The most widely available cultivar is *E. alpinum* 'Superbum', a glorious plant, more vigorous than the species, and available as seed.

Many gardeners refer to sea holly as 'Miss Willmott's Ghost', but actually this applies only to one species, *E. giganteum*. Native to eastern Europe and growing to a height of 36 inches (90 centimeters), this species tends to be a biennial or a short-lived perennial. These days, Ellen Willmott is remembered chiefly for the company she kept (Gertrude Jekyll, Mrs. C.W. "Theresa" Earle and William Robinson were among her friends), as a plantswoman, and for this species of sea holly.

The story goes that she so admired the very large silvery-gray flowers that this plant produces, she actually used to surreptitiously scatter seeds of it throughout the borders of the gardens she visited. Within a year or two, the sea holly would flower, and it soon became clear that the mystery plants all had one thing in common — they dwelt in the gardens that Ellen Willmott frequented — hence, Miss Willmott's Ghost.

Ellen Willmott was the only woman other than Gertrude Jekyll to receive the Victoria Medal of Honour, but the gardens that she created were much more elaborate than those bearing the Jekyll stamp. Gardening at Warley Place in Essex, she inherited a vast fortune, which she eventually squandered on her passion for horticulture, in the end losing both fortune and gardens. Let that be a lesson to us all!

Finally, it would be remiss to leave the eryngiums without mentioning rattlesnake master (*E. yuccifolium*). Native to the eastern United States, this is a plant that you either love or hate. Quite different in appearance to the sea hollies, rattlesnake master has sword-shaped blue-gray leaves and bears pale green flowers during late summer. I always think that *E. yuccifolium* would look better in a southwestern style garden than in my cottage garden. It also looks great in wildflower or prairie gardens.

NAME: Sea holly *Eryngium* spp. and cultivars

HEIGHT: 2 to 3' (60 to 90 cm)

EXPOSURE: Sun to part sun

BLOOMING PERIOD: Summer

SOIL: Ordinary to rich garden soil

COMPANIONS: Goes marvelously well with the pale yellow flowers of giant scabious (*Cephalaria gigantea*) or the pale pink of *Centaurea dealbata*

SPECIAL NOTES: A solid "architectural" plant that resembles a shrub by mid-summer

Verbascum

 Verbascum spp. and cultivars

VERBASCUMS CAN BE added to the list of perennial plants that lend valuable vertical accents and height to the cottage garden. Often known as "mullein" (from the Norman *moleine*, itself a corruption of the Latin *mollis*, meaning "soft"), most species are native to Eurasia and require a location in full to part sun in ordinary garden soil.

By far the most well-known species of verbascum is common mullein (*V. thapsus*). Familiar to North Americans from Alaska to Florida, this introduction is now considered a weed in most parts of the continent. It re-colonized Britain after the end of the last Ice Age and is generally considered a native species. Common mullein is a tall, striking plant hardy to zone 2, and bearing tall spikes (up to 6 feet/1.8 meters) of yellow flowers that arise from large wooly leaves whose texture is reminiscent of lamb's ears (*Stachys byzantina*).

Long used for bronchial conditions both in animal and human populations, *V. thapsus* has recently been shown to contain anti-tubercular substances, proving that occasionally there is more than a grain of wisdom in some of the old herbal remedies. In his volume *Adam in Eden* (1657), Coles advises that "husbandmen of Kent do give it their cattle against the cough of the lungs, and I, therefore, mention it because cattle are also in some sort to be provided for in their diseases." Because of its widespread medicinal use, common mullein became a fixture in early cottage gardens, and most of the romantic Victorian watercolors include it.

In spite of its being reported in many texts as fundamental to the style, I'm reticent to recommend it to home gardeners. A biennial by habit, common mullein produces vast quantities of seed after flowering, and a single plant may give rise to hundreds of seedlings. Vita Sackville-West concurs and adds, "It seeds itself everywhere, and becomes a nuisance and a problem, because in good conditions it is almost too handsome a weed to root out." In other words, "Cottage gardeners beware, and deadhead assiduously if you intend to grow this species."

A far more well-behaved and naturally perennial verbascum is the nettle-leaved mullein (*V. chaixii*). It's native to eastern Europe and was introduced into British gardens in 1821. It took a few years for this verbascum to grow on me, but grow on me it did! Hardy to zone 4, *V. chaixii* develop 3-foot (90 centimeter) spikes from a semi-evergreen basal rosette, densely packed with small butter-yellow flowers replete with mauve eyes, which, when in bloom, are covered with docile neighborhood bees. In rich soils, this sun-loving plant may need staking, perhaps from the weight of the foraging insects as much

---

Verbascum phoeniceum **Hybrids Hardy to Zone 4**

Cotswold Queen – (1935) Pale yellow flowers with purple filaments

Gainsborough – Primrose yellow flowers

Helen Johnson – Coppery orange with a splash of cream

Lilac Domino – Spikes of pure lilac

Mont Blanc – As the name suggests, pristine white flowers

Pink Domino – Deep rose-pink flowers with dark purple filaments

Southern Charm – A dwarf cultivar mix (height to 12"/30 cm) in an excellent range of pastel shades

Requiring only average garden soil, the drought-tolerant Verbascum *clan should have at least a few representatives in every North American cottage garden. Rather than including the traditional (and invasive) common mullein (*V. thapsus*), concentrate on seeking out nettle-leaved (*V. chaixii*) and purple (*V. phoeniceum*) mullein cultivars. Hardy to zone 3, dark mullein (*V. nigrum*) is also an excellent candidate for cottage garden culture.*

as anything. If you grow it on leaner soils, it won't flop, nor will it grow quite so tall. Even more beautiful is the white form of this mullein, *V. chaixii* 'Album', still sporting its characteristic mauve eye.

Purple mullein (*V. phoeniceum*) was one of the first plants I ever grew from seed. In spite of its reputation as a short-lived perennial, many of my plants are over a decade old. Growing in average garden soil in full sun, this mullein sends up 2- to 3-foot (60 to 90 centimeter) flowering spikes from beautifully textured dark green basal rosettes. Some strains apparently produce much taller plants (up to 4 feet/120 centimeters) but I've never seen them myself. Flowering in late spring, they always seem to me to be a prelude to the summer delphiniums, having much in common with them structurally.

Native to Eurasia, and hardy to zone 3, purple mullein was introduced into cultivation in 1796. The common name of this verbascum is something of a misnomer, since purple is just the beginning. Plants grown from seed will produce saucer-shaped blooms of pure white, pink, violet, dark purple, and everything in-between, often with a contrasting eye. If you want to encourage a perennial habit, deadheading is important, but as with lupines, I usually leave a few seed capsules on plants so that I get some new color combinations every spring.

If you find you have a plant whose blooms you are particularly fond of, and you don't want to lose it, it's quite easy to propagate verbascum clonally from root cuttings taken from offshoots or sections of the long taproot after flowering and grown on in pots. Successful cuttings can then be planted out in the garden in the autumn. As well as being available as a mix of colors, purple mullein seed can also be purchased in individual colors such as 'Flush of White' which usually blooms the first year. Subsequent generations may produce a more varied palette.

During the 1930s, extensive crossing of *V. phoeniceum* with some of the yellow-flowered species produced a race of cultivars called Cotswold hybrids. The first of these, 'Cotswold Queen' (1935), produced quite a stir, and many more have been introduced since then. As lovely as they are, these plants truly are short-lived perennials, having inherited that tendency from the biennial habit of their yellow-flowered parents. Hardy to zone 4, these hybrids are somewhat taller and denser than purple mullein, attaining heights of 4 feet (120 centimeters), and occasionally requiring staking as a result, especially in exposed locations.

Writing in 1937 when these new hybrids were brand new, an enthusiastic Vita Sackville-West felt that "it does not much matter which variety you specify, for they are all equally desirable. They are all dusty, fusty, musty in coloring – queer colors, to which it is impossible to give a definite name: they are neither pink, nor yellow, nor coral, nor apricot, but a cloudy mixture between all those."

Cottage gardeners everywhere will sympathize with Vita's lament, bemoaning the fact that her mulleins required some seasonal ministrations:

"The lupins [*sic*] stand heavy with seed-pods and so do the delphiniums, but where are the necessary two, three, four hours to come from? What chance for the verbascum, who are less showy but more subtle and quite as deserving?"

NAME: Verbascum *Verbascum* spp. and cultivars

HEIGHT: To 6' (1.8 m) – cultivars usually shorter

EXPOSURE: Sun to part sun

BLOOMING PERIOD: Summer

SOIL: Ordinary to rich garden soil

COMPANIONS: Great with ❦obedient plant (*Physostegia virginiana*), which blooms later in the season, as does ❦Joe Pye weed (*Eupatorium purpureum*)

SPECIAL NOTES: Let a few plants self seed to ensure future generations and different color combinations

---

❧ No Cottage Garden Should Be Without One

Needless to say, there are lots of insouciant, low-maintenance perennials that will add interest and excitement to your cottage garden. Here are 20 suggestions to get you started.

Balloon flower (*Platycodon grandiflorus*) Zone 4

Bearded iris (*Iris* spp. and cultivars) Zones 3–4

❦Blazing star (*Liatris spicata*) Zone 4

❦Bottle gentian (*Gentiana andrewsii*) Zone 4

Christmas rose (*Helleborus niger*) Zone 4

❦Columbine (some) (*Aquilegia* spp.) Zones 3–4

❦Coral bells (*Heuchera americana* and cultivars) Zone 4

Cupid's dart (*Catananche caerulea*) Zone 3

❦Foam flower (*Tiarella* spp. and cultivars) Zones 3–4

Globe thistle (*Echinops ritro*) Zone 3

Herbaceous clematis (*Clematis integrifolia*) Zones 4–5

Lungwort (*Pulmonaria* spp. and cultivars) Zones 4–5

❦Michaelmas daisy (*Aster novi-belgii* and cultivars) Zone 4

Peony (*Paeonia* spp. and cultivars) Zones 3–4

Pinks (*Dianthus* spp. and cultivars) Zones 3–4

❦Phlox (*Phlox* spp. and cultivars) Zone 4

Plantain lily (*Hosta plantaginea* and cultivars) Zone 3

Rose campion (*Lychnis coronaria*) Zone 4

Shasta daisy (*Leucanthemum* x *superbum*) Zone 5

Yarrow (*Achillea* spp. and cultivars) Zones 3–4

❦ = native

CHAPTER FIVE

Bulbs

I HAVE YET TO MEET a gardener who doesn't love bulbs. Nothing is more indicative of spring's arrival than flowering bulbs, and cottage gardeners should always leave plenty of room for these seasonal charmers. Once the bulbs have finished, their growing spaces can be switched over to the cultivation of annual herbs, flowers and vegetables.

In addition, there are many summer flowering bulbs that some gardeners tend to overlook. Summer flowering bulbs are generally from warm climates and as a result require lifting and storage indoors over the winter months in colder areas. This puts lots of people off, but the operation is a simple one, providing that you can provide a cool, dark spot in your home. The corner of an unfinished basement or root cellar works very well, and if you can close any nearby heat vents, so much the better.

"Bulbs" is a bit of a blanket term that encompasses true bulbs, corms and tubers. Recently the term *geophyte* has been introduced to include not only bulbs, but also herbaceous plants with fleshy underground structures whose primary role is to store food and water. Many of our native North American plants fall into this last category, such as bloodroot, jack-in-the-pulpit and trillium.

Crocus, daffodils, tulips and alliums will likely make up the lion's share of your bulb purchases in any given year, but it's well worthwhile ferreting out some of the less well known bulbs. They will add extra interest and color to your garden, while at the same time extending your season of bloom and augmenting flexibility within your borders.

When purchasing spring flowering bulbs, bear in mind that some bloom early in the season, while others bloom much later. Try to get a good selection of both types — you'll extend your flowering period by several weeks. Pictured here is an early-blooming Kaufmanniana *tulip with* Narcissus *'Dove Wings' (introduced 1949).*

Winter aconite

Eranthis spp.

WINTER ACONITE IS among the most delightful of the early spring bulbs and is preceded only by the common snowdrop (*Galanthus nivalis*). In some areas they may even bloom together, and it's not unusual to see the heads of both, bravely poking through a final blanket of winter snow.

Members of the buttercup family and hardy to zone 4, these diminutive jewels have golden yellow buttercup-like flowers that are framed by glossy green sepals, looking like Elizabethan collar ruffs. Because it grows only 2 to 4 inches (5 to 10 centimeters) high, it's necessary to plant winter aconite where it can be easily seen, near the house or a walkway. Given time and the right conditions, aconite will spread to form a golden carpet while your earliest crocuses are just beginning to send up tentative green spikes.

Winter aconite can be naturalized in lawns or planted under deciduous shrubs and trees. They don't do well under the denser shade provided by evergreens and prefer alkaline soil when given the choice. In the open garden, aconites will thrive, providing they aren't disturbed by heavy cultivation later in the season.

A classic combination is to plant winter aconite with Christmas roses (*Helleborus niger*), another member of the buttercup family, which may be in bloom at the same time. I also grow them in a section of the garden that is heavily planted with primroses and auricula, and this also works very well—the primulas taking over nicely once the aconite has faded. Both genera like the same conditions: moist, humus-rich soil with part sun early in the season that leafs out into part shade by the time spring is giving way to summer. A patch of "evergreen" black mondo grass (*Ophiopogon planiscapus* 'Nigrescens') has crept into the area, and the gold of the aconite against the black strap-shaped leaves of the mondo grass make a dramatic statement indeed.

Another option is to plant them where selfseeding annuals will take over by mid to late spring. Johnny-jump-up and love-in-a-mist both suit this purpose admirably and can be ripped out in autumn without disturbing the shallow tubers of winter aconite.

There are three species of aconite with which we should concern ourselves. The first is *Eranthis hyemalis* or European aconite. Native from Bulgaria to the south of France, this species has naturalized for centuries across Britain and is likely the best known. It is the first of the aconites to bloom, the flowers being marginally smaller than in other species. *Eranthis hyemalis* sets seed easily and spreads quickly, especially in moist climates.

Eranthis cilicica or Turkish aconite is very similar to European aconite. It has slightly larger flowers and blooms 7 to 10 days later than the standard form. Rather than a glossy green ruff, Turkish aconite has a bronze tinge to its foliage, which is also more finely dissected. While *E. cilicica* doesn't spread as rapidly as *E. hyemalis*, it is considerably more tolerant of hot, dry summers.

A cross between European and Turkish aconite has resulted in a cultivar known as *Eranthis* x *tubergenii* 'Guinea Gold', which was bred by the Dutch firm of van Tubergen (see how easy it is to have a plant named after you?). Bearing flowers larger than either of its parents, it flowers about one week after Turkish aconite. Some gardeners will prefer this plant since it is sterile, and, lacking the ability to self-seed, is consequently credited with possessing a tidier habit. Clumps will increase slowly as underground tubers expand in both size and number, but all reproduction will be vegetative or asexual.

So with all this going for it, why isn't winter aconite grown more widely? The answer is easy: although it's a simple plant to cultivate once it's established, it can be difficult to get it going initially. This isn't the fault of the gardener, nor does it seem fitting to blame the plant itself. The trouble is that aconite is one of the few geophytes that prefers to be moved or transplanted "in the green" — in other words while it's in active growth. Since this event occurs so early in the gardening season and lasts only a couple of weeks, the whole concept is fraught with problems for growers, distributors and buyers. The window of opportunity is simply too small.

As a result, winter aconite tubers are usually offered in the autumn with the bulk of the other spring bulbs, when they are completely dormant and desiccated, and looking like last year's sultanas. This is not the ideal scenario if it's high germination rates you're after. To overcome these obstacles, the tubers should be re-hydrated for several hours (preferably in a diluted transplant solution, e.g., 10–52–10) until they look a little plumper. Some guides recommend a 24-hour soak before planting, but this is excessive, and cuts the tuber off from oxygen for far too long. After soaking, the tubers should immediately be planted 2 to 3 inches (5 to 7.5 centimeters) below the soil surface. If they aren't planted directly after soaking, they will very likely start to rot. Whatever you do, don't agonize about planting them right-side up — even the experts can't tell, but fortunately, the tubers themselves know which way is up.

Often seen poking up through a final blanket of snow, the irresistible blooms of winter aconite (Eranthis spp.) are preceded only by the snowdrop (Galanthus spp.). The key to successful cultivation of this species is simple: purchase the tiny tubers as soon as they become available (late summer or early autumn), soak them in a diluted transplant solution for several hours, and then plant them immediately.

Luckily the tubers aren't expensive so I always buy at least 50, plant them quite densely, and am happy if I get good results from 25. Just remember that once they take hold, you'll have them forever.

Perhaps Northamptonshire poet John Clare (1793–1864) summed aconite up best when he wrote:

> . . . The winter aconite,
> With buttercup-like flowers, that shut at night;
> Its green leaf furling round its cup of gold,
> Like tender maiden muffled from the cold.

NAME: Winter aconite *Eranthis* species

HEIGHT: 2 to 4" (5 to 10 cm)

EXPOSURE: Sun

BLOOMING PERIOD: Late winter to early spring

SOIL: Rich soil with good drainage

COMPANIONS: Blooming so early, winter aconite hasn't any floral competition except from snowdrops (*Galanthus* spp.).

SPECIAL NOTES: Best planted around perennials where the shallow tubers can remain undisturbed. Excellent in conjunction with hellebores (*Helleborus* spp.) or ❦blazing star (*Liatris spicata*).

Bloodroot

Sanguinaria canadensis

BLOODROOT IS ONE of the most captivating of the spring geophytes, and no North American cottage garden should be considered complete without it. Because it's native to North America, it would not have been found in English cottage gardens – but it's just the type of indigenous plant those cottagers would have loved. A member of the poppy family, bloodroot is the only known species of the *Sanguinaria* genera and is native from Nova Scotia south to Florida, and as far west as Texas, north through Kansas to Manitoba. Hardy to zone 3, bloodroot is listed as an endangered or threatened species in some states, which should be reason enough to grow it, but it is the chaste white blooms that attract most gardeners.

In early to mid spring, tightly furled gray-green leaves arise from a tangle of rhizomes, piercing the soil surface. Emerging from the leaves is a pale pink bud, which will slowly swell and then finally burst open to reveal eight delicate white petals surrounding golden yellow stamens. Until the flower is fertilized, the leaves will stay folded around the bloom protecting it from extremes of wind and cold. Once the flower is fertilized, the handsome cloak of foliage will unfurl, revealing a bold outline similar to that of a fig leaf.

In its natural habitat, bloodroot is a resident of the forest floor, so in a garden situation, it will require plenty of organic matter and leaf mold. It prefers part to full shade; the leaves will turn yellow and drop off if the plant gets too much sun or is allowed to dry out during the heat of summer.

Bloodroot tolerates either acidic or alkaline soil and associates admirably with other plants suitable for shady locations. In addition to increasing vegetatively through rhizomes, the species also sets seed. Each individual seed has a small fleshy appendage that ants find irresistible. As the ants gather the seeds to take them back to their nest, they are actually serving as mobile dispensing units, ensuring that the seed is scattered far and wide.

Bloodroot acquired its common name because when the rhizomes are cut, they exude a brownish-red to orange sap. It is this alkaloid-rich sap that was prized by native Americans and early settlers to relieve a variety of maladies. Another common name for bloodroot is "red puccoon," from the Amerindian word *pak*, which referred to plants that were used for dyeing cloth. The juice of the roots was also used to dye baskets and for war paint.

Writing in 1612 about his experiences at Jamestown, Virginia, Captain John Smith noted, "This they use for swellings, aches, anointing their joints, painting their heads and garments." It didn't exactly end there though, since he goes on to say "they set a woman fresh-painted red to be a bedfellow" of one of the colonists. In the Ponca tribe, a young man would rub the palm of his hand with bloodroot sap as a love potion, and then endeavor to shake hands with the woman he desired. After shaking hands, the bachelor could expect the woman to fall under his spell within five or six days.

The juice itself is extremely caustic and capable of destroying tissue. Early settlers employed it as an expectorant for clearing the respiratory tract, and it was listed as such in the *U.S. Pharmacopoeia* from 1820 to 1926. Nevertheless, bloodroot is a poison that in larger doses will cause tunnel vision and vomiting, and the United States' Food and Drug Administration now lists bloodroot as "unsafe." In spite of this,

*One of the most extravagant springtime displays in twenty-first-century cottage gardens will inevitably be that of our native North American bloodroot (*Sanguinaria canadensis*). Discovered as a natural mutation near Dayton, Ohio, in 1916, the 60-petalled 'Multiplex' (pictured here) must be lifted and divided about every four years to maintain vigor and discourage root rot.*

NAME: ❀Bloodroot *Sanguinaria canadensis*
HEIGHT: 6 to 8" (15 to 20 cm)
EXPOSURE: Shade to part sun
BLOOMING PERIOD: Spring
SOIL: Moist and rich in organic matter
COMPANIONS: Wonderful with ❀Virginia bluebells (*Mertensia pulmonarioides*) and ❀*Trillium* spp.
SPECIAL NOTES: Divide large clumps every 3 to 4 years

the main alkaloid present in the plant, *sanguinarine*, has shown anticancer and antiseptic properties in the laboratory, and a chemically refined form is used commercially as a plaque-inhibiting agent in toothpastes and mouthwashes.

In addition to the usual single form of bloodroot, there are two other types gardeners should be on the lookout for. A semi-double form with up to 16 petals was isolated as early as 1732 by German botanist Johann Dillenius and is sometimes offered as *Sanguinaria* 'Flore Pleno'. This mutation appears fairly regularly in the wild, and if you allow your plants to self-seed, it's quite conceivable you'll find one or two specimens in your own garden after a number of years.

Unquestionably, the belle of the bloodroot ball is the 60-petalled *Sanguinaria* 'Multiplex'. With pure white flowers that look similar to those of a water lily (*Nymphaea* spp.), 'Multiplex' steals the show with blooms that last even longer than those of the standard form. This mutation was first discovered growing wild near Dayton, Ohio, in 1916. Specimens were promptly sent to the Arnold Arboretum in Boston, from which all subsequent plants have been propagated.

Unfortunately, these very double types are sterile and won't self-seed, the stamens having assumed an asexual petal-like form. As a result, they must be propagated vegetatively by division and are therefore considerably more expensive to purchase. 'Multiplex' is a vigorous plant, but in order to keep it robust, the rhizomes must be lifted and separated every four years or so. Otherwise the tangle of roots become too congested, rot will set in, and the entire clump may perish. Plants should be divided in late summer or autumn, before the foliage disappears.

Camas

Camassia spp.

MANY GARDENERS CONSIDER that camas is the North American equivalent to the English bluebell (*Hyacinthoides non-scripta*), and certainly both belong to the lily family and have a similar appearance, although camas bloom somewhat later than bluebells do and prefer a more open situation than at the base of deciduous trees where bluebells like to make their home. And, if anything, when judged on individual merit, the camas is a considerably more striking plant.

Sadly, camas represents yet another group of native plants that suffer from tremendous underexposure, and being as carefree as they are, it's hard to understand why. Occurring naturally in the alpine meadows of the Rocky Mountains from British Columbia south to California, and inland as far as Montana and Utah, great colonies of plants bloom in early summer to coincide with the floods produced by the late spring mountain runoff.

Available in shades of deep purple through pale blue to white, these thoroughly enchanting plants are often recommended for part shade locations. Given their choice, they prefer full sun in rich soil that stays consistently moist at least until blooming time. After that, it doesn't seem to matter if the soil dries out since they quickly go dormant in any case. I plant them beneath New England asters (*Aster novae-angliae*) that are just beginning to hit their stride as the camas fades, effectively hiding their maturing foliage. They will tolerate part shade, but may sometimes flop under less than sunny conditions.

Looking back, when I first received camas bulbs as a gift (a great way to indoctrinate the uninitiated), they were simply labeled *Camassia*. Although I now recognize them as *C. leichtlinii*, you may experience the same slipshod labeling at your local garden center. Don't worry too much about it: whatever the species of camas you purchase, you're guaranteed to love the results. Available in the autumn with other spring-blooming geophytes, camas bulbs should be planted as soon as possible, since they need sufficient time to send out roots before the ground freezes. Many authorities list very disparate hardiness zones for camas, but most of this information is erroneous. As a rule, camas bulbs are hardy to zone 4, and given a little winter mulch, to zone 3. All *Camassias* make excellent cut flowers.

The name camas is a corruption of the Amerindian name for the plant, *quamash*. Camas was an important food source for native North Americans, but I don't recommend you attempt to feast on garden varieties of the plant. A fourth species known as Eastern camas (*C. scilloides*) is the most palatable of the genus, and this is the plant that was widely consumed. Native from southern Ontario and the Great Lake states to as far south as Texas (and generally growing west of the

Other Camas Species

If you are lucky enough to be able to select individual species and cultivars of camas, here's what you should know about them.

1. Common camas (*C. quamash*) — Native to southern Alberta and British Columbia, south to Montana and Oregon. Perhaps the easiest species to grow, and certainly enjoying the widest natural distribution, this camas tends to flop unless grown in full sun. Ranging in color from white to deep blue, look for the cultivars 'Orion' and 'San Juan'. Maximum height, 24" (60 cm).

2. Cusick camas (*C. cusickii*) — From Oregon, with bulbs weighing up to a half-pound (250 g). Height to 30" (75 cm) with pale blue flowers. 'Zwanenburg' (deep blue flowers) is the best-known cultivar and was introduced by the Dutch firm of van Tubergen before World War I.

3. Great camas (*C. leichtlinii*) — Native from British Columbia south to California, this camas has received more attention than other species from plant breeders. The very rare white form (occurring at a rate of 1 in 10,000 plants) was the first of this species to be discovered and is therefore regarded as the true type, although shades of blue are obviously 10,000 times more common in the wild. In spite of this, two recessive white types are available: 'Alba', with bright white flowers, and 'Semiplena', a semi-double form with cream-colored blooms. 'Blue Danube' (or *Blau Donau*) is an old variety with violet flowers; height to 36" (90 cm).

Appalachians), the bulbs are reminiscent of sweet onions. Boiled for 25 to 30 minutes or wrapped in foil and baked at 350°F (170°C) for 45 minutes, they add a unique flavor to meals for those of you given to gastronomic investigation. Slightly gummy in texture when cooked, the sugar-rich bulbs also yield a sort of molasses, which was used by American Indians on festive occasions. Upon reaching the Oregon Territory in 1804, William Clark and Meriwether Lewis were served baked camas, for which I'm certain they were thankful, given some of the alternatives.

Camassia species crossed the ocean during the early years of Victoria's reign and ironically have been adopted by English cottage gardeners as if they had been there from the start. In 1914, E. A. Bowles boasted that "some very good *Camassia* seedlings are taking their [Fritillaries] place. The first I planted were some named seedlings of *C. leichtlinii*, a pure white and a very deep purple called Purple Robe; now seedlings have appeared in all directions, and some are of a very good deep blue and purple shades."

Camas have also assumed their rightful place in

Requiring moist soil conditions during active spring growth, our native camas (Camassia spp.) can give any English bluebell (Hyacinthoides non-scripta) a floral run for its money. It has leaves that hang around somewhat longer than most gardeners would like, so it's a good idea to over-plant camas bulbs with herbaceous perennials (Geranium, ❦Heuchera and ❦Aster spp. work well) to conceal the maturing camas foliage.

NAME: ❦Camas *Camassia* species and cultivars
HEIGHT: 2 to 3' (60 to 90 cm)
EXPOSURE: Sun to part sun
BLOOMING PERIOD: Late spring
SOIL: Ordinary to rich garden soil
COMPANIONS: Contrasts well with mourning widow
   (*Geranium phaem*), which blooms at the same time,
   and can be over-planted with the diminutive
   geophyte *Brimeura amethystina*
SPECIAL NOTES: Adequate soil moisture during the
   early spring months is essential for good bloom.

that other great British garden, Hidcote Manor, no doubt installed by the fair hand of farsighted Gertrude Jekyll. Now they've naturalized all over the estate. I believe that amounts to being horticulturally acceptable in the very highest circles. And not a moment too soon.

Four o'clocks

Mirabilis jalapa

I NEVER CEASE to be amazed when visiting gardeners (who ought to know better) stop and stare in amazement at my four o'clocks. "But what are they?" they exclaim. I always feel somewhat embarrassed by this and generally mutter a barely audible "*Mirabilis*" in response. Why be shy? Well, it's a little like someone telling you your shasta daisies are exquisite, or that your petunias are the most beautiful thing they've ever seen. You see, four o'clocks are the easiest plants in the world to grow, but instead of being considered prosaic, they appear to have been elevated to loftier heights and now enjoy a rather rarified status.

The plant's other common name 'Marvel of Peru' speaks of its origins in tropical South America. Hardy to zone 8 or 9, and requiring a full sun location, it is a perennial plant in its natural environment. In northern areas it is often treated as an annual (it blooms the first year from seed), or as a drought-tolerant tender bulb. I prefer the latter designation because most gardeners will lift the large turnip-like tubers after the first frosts and store them indoors in a cool, dark place over winter.

Four o'clocks are so called because like the moonflower (*Ipomoea alba*), they open in the late afternoon or early evening, and close the following morning when the sun hits them. I love a plant that *does* something, and between the morning glories, the evening primroses (*Oenothera triloba*) and the four o'clocks, I'm really spoiled for choice. Add to that a gentle sweet scent, and you get the picture.

In addition to opening and closing on cue, four o'clocks have another unusual feature, and that is their petals, or rather, the lack thereof. The "flowering" parts of the plant are, in fact, sepals, and not petals. Sepals usually enclose and protect the flower bud, and the easiest way to picture this is to think of a rose. Before opening, the petals are covered by green petal-like structures, which are the sepals. Sepals are referred to collectively as the calyx, and it is for this unique, colorful calyx that we grow four o'clocks. A "flowering calyx" is characteristic of all members of the four o'clock family (Nyctaginaceae), and that other well-known member of the clan, bougainvillea, behaves in precisely the same way.

The other interesting feature of the calyx is that the pigment is set down in layers, one color on top of the other, and this gives the flowers a strangely luminescent quality. And colorful they are, coming in bizarre combinations of red, pink, magenta, yellow and white, frequently with several colors mottled or streaked together on a solid background. If you save your tubers from one year to the next, you can select and keep only those colors you really like. I tend to save the more exotic-looking combinations, and also start some fresh seed every spring to see what new colors I can come up with. Many gardeners covet the pure white form of *Mirabilis*, as it's visible from quite a distance, especially in the moonlight. This makes perfect botanical sense as four o'clocks are pollinated by hummingbirds as the sun begins to set, and then by night-flying moths later in the evening.

Mirabilis comes from the Latin for "wonderful" or "remarkable," and this seems an appropriate name, considering the number of acrobatics that four o'clocks are capable of performing. *Jalapa* is Latin for Xalapa, a town in Mexico where the purgative drug *jalap* was first discovered. Four o'clock tubers were sometimes substituted for the genuine *jalap*, which comes from an entirely unrelated plant, *Exogonium jalapa*.

Four o'clocks were first discovered by Europeans during the Spanish conquest of Central America and northern South America from 1511 to 1530. In addition to marigolds (*Tagetes* spp.) and nasturtiums (*Tropaeolum* spp.), the conquistadors also brought back *Mirabilis jalapa*. Four o'clocks had definitely made their way into English gardens before the sixteenth century ended. In 1597, Gerard waxed poetic about them for several of the most entertaining pages in his entire *Herball*. In Europe, these plants have always been more commonly called Marvel of Peru, but Gerard goes one step further and asserts that "in English rather the Marvell of the World, than of Peru alone."

Graham Stuart Thomas recommends four o'clocks as suitable plants for commuters who only spend their evenings at home, and this seems to me to be a very sensible notion. In addition to sun, the one thing that they require in order to flourish is heat. Don't plant seedlings outside, or direct seed into the open ground until the soil has really warmed up — once again, use the tomato planting-out date as a guide. As soon as the requisite heat is supplied, the plants take off. They grow so quickly that in warm regions such as the southern states I've even seen them used as a low annual hedge.

First-year tubers are available in the spring along with other tender geophytes, but seed is the easiest and most inexpensive way to get acquainted with these foolproof plants, and usually it will be offered simply as *Mirabilis jalapa*. There are, however, two cultivars worth looking out for. The first is 'Four O'Clock Special', a multicolored type with plenty of streaking and mottling, height to 24 inches (60 centimeters). The second is 'Jingles', which is also variously spotted and flecked in a good range of colors, height to 30 inches (75 centimeters).

In most parts of North America, four o'clocks will start to bloom by the beginning of August and will keep going strong until the end of September, and another big plus: they don't need to be deadheaded. I have them planted with *Lilium speciosum* var. *rubrum* (introduced 1873), which bloom at the same time, adding depth and texture to the Easter egg colors of the four o'clocks. For the critics in the crowd, I try to chill it all out with purple perilla and silver artemisia.

NAME: Four o'clocks *Mirabilis jalapa*

HEIGHT: 2 to 3' (60 to 90 cm)

EXPOSURE: Sun

BLOOMING PERIOD: Summer to early autumn

SOIL: Ordinary to rich garden soil

COMPANIONS: Stand well by themselves, but are also lovely when punctuated with the spikes of *Lobelia* x *speciosa* cultivars such as the 'Compliment' or 'Fan' series. Also associates well with *Ageratum houstonianum* cultivars, and 'Blue Horizon' in particular.

SPECIAL NOTES: Night blooming and sweet-scented, tubers may be over-wintered in a cool basement

Snake's-head fritillary

Fritillaria meleagris

THE *FRITILLARIA* GENUS comprises about one hundred species of bulbous perennials, at least a third of which have been cultivated in gardens at one time or another, with varying degrees of success. The most flamboyant and widely grown of these is undoubtedly the Crown Imperial (*Fritillaria imperialis*), native to the Himalayan ranges of Kashmir where I spent my childhood, and where great drifts of these plants were taken for granted as part of the annual springtime ritual. They also have a long history of cultivation in the cottage garden, having been introduced to England by 1582.

Other species are native to China and Japan, much of Europe, and even the Pacific Coast of our own continent. Unfortunately, most of our native species are very choosy about location, as they are intricately adapted to their individual microclimates. Most don't make very good garden subjects unless they are grown in a region where they are indigenous. Sad but true.

Of much more mysterious origin is the snake's-head fritillary. Botanists have been arguing for years over whether this plant is actually native to Britain or not. Incredibly, the first record of snake's-head fritillary occurring in the wild dates only from 1736, although it was grown in gardens long before this (Gerard mentions it as early 1597). Before the opening of the North Sea channel (*c.* 5500 BC), the Rhine and the Thames formed part of a single river system, and it is in the Rhine region where the most concentrated wild populations still exist. It therefore seems likely that snake's-head fritillary would have been present in postglacial Britain.

Interestingly, the entire genus was named for the physical attributes of snake's-head fritillary alone. *Fritillus* is Latin for "dice box," referring to the checkered pattern of the flower, and its boxy, bell shape, and as if to reinforce the idea, *meleagris* is derived from the Greek for "guinea-hen," whose feathers are marked with the same pattern.

Aside from being one of the most beautiful fritillaries, the snake's-head is also the easiest to cultivate in the widest range of garden situations. Hardy to zone 3, it requires a moist situation in sun to part shade, with reasonably rich soil. Growing naturally in wet meadows like the camas, it requires plenty of moisture up until flowering time, but once the slight foliage has matured the dormant bulb will tolerate the drier conditions of high summer.

Usually reaching a height of about 12 inches (30 centimeters), *F. meleagris* has gray-green foliage and

---

~ Other Names for *Fritillaria*

Further evidence that snake's-head fritillary has a long association with Britain is obvious by the number of local country names assigned to the plant:

Bloody warrior (each plant supposedly springing from a drop of Dane's blood) — Berkshire
Chequered lily (for its checker-board markings) — Somerset
Drooping bell of Sodom — Dorset
Guinea-hen flower (referring to the resemblance of the checkered markings of the feathers) — Cumbria
Leper's lily (a reference to the similarly-shaped bells that lepers were required to wear to warn of their approach) — Devonshire
Weeping widow — Staffordshire

bears one or two pendant bell-shaped flowers in various shades of purple to pure white, usually with a checkered pattern. In England, snake's-head fritillary is often naturalized in grass, but to do this effectively takes a few thousand bulbs and several decades, so I have never attempted anything on so grand a scale. Nevertheless, these plants take up no space at all and are so slender that they can be festooned throughout your borders wherever conditions are right. Over time they will self-seed, but as is the case with so many small bulbs, the difficulty is establishing them initially. Again, this is due to the fact that there is always a lag from the time the bulbs are harvested until they make their way into your hot hands with the rest of the fall bulb glut. *F. meleagris* can suffer severely from desiccation, so it's vital that the bulbs be purchased the moment they're available and then planted promptly. Unlike winter aconite, once dried out, these bulbs can't be revived.

There is a widespread misconception that fritillaries should be planted on their sides, since all bulbs of this genus have a depression where the flowering stalk arises. The idea is that water collects in this cavity, causing the bulbs to rot. Nothing could be further from the truth. All geophytes have contractile roots — that is, they are capable of pulling themselves down through the soil, or turning themselves right side up. In botanical terms, this makes perfect sense: how else would a bulbous plant that begins life as a seed on the soil's surface, ever become a large bulb firmly lodged a foot or more down? The answer is simple: the bulb-ette forms contractile roots that pull the structure down to its chosen depth. In the same way, any bulb planted on its side or upside down will quickly right itself. Some gardeners make a great deal of fuss about planting geophytes at the correct depth, but regardless of how deep you plant them, if they survive the first season or two, you can be sure that they will have traveled to the depth that suits them best. Isn't that reassuring?

I dote on snake's-head fritillary and would encourage you to give it a try. Bulbs are reasonably priced, so don't plant fewer than 15 or 20 in a single clump, lest they look lonely. If at the same time should you spy *Fritillaria michailovskyi* (sorry, no common name — think Mikhail Baryshnikov), by all means grab it. Almost as carefree as the snake's-head, this fritillary is native to Turkey and hardy to zone 4. A completely charming and diminutive plant, it blooms just after *F. meleagris*, and is slightly shorter at 6 to 8 inches (15 to 20 centimeters). And no history lessons here — *F. michailovskyi* wasn't discovered until 1905, and it wasn't until 1965 when bulb guru Brian Mathew reintroduced it that it began to be cultivated in gardens. Up to seven pendant flowers per stem of deep metallic purple with upturned yellow tips. Gorgeous!

↶ A Plant for Poets

Although Vita Sackville-West felt that the snake's-head fritillary was both familiar and foreign at once, I've never seen it myself. She writes the following descriptive lines in her epic bucolic poem *The Land*:

And then I came to a field where the springing grass
Was dulled by the hanging cups of fritillaries,
Sullen and foreign-looking, the snaky flower,
Scarfed in dull purple, like Egyptian girls
Camping among the furze, staining the waste
With foreign colour, sulky-dark and quaint . . .

NAME: Snake's-head fritillary *Fritillaria meleagris*
HEIGHT: To 12" (30 cm)
EXPOSURE: Sun to part sun
BLOOMING PERIOD: Spring
SOIL: Ordinary to rich garden soil
COMPANIONS: Associates well with ❧ shooting star (*Dodecatheon meadia*) and ❧ wild ginger (*Asarum canadense*)
SPECIAL NOTES: Buy bulbs as soon as they become available and plant immediately

The checkered patterns of snake's-head fritillary are captivating in the extreme and invite some serious micro-inspection. Garden writer Beverley Nichols (1898–1983) frequently alluded to the fact that the very best gardeners are well-practiced in the art of "shrinking." If you're capable of reducing yourself to the size of a grain of rice, by all means do so — you'll be amazed at the startling new vistas Fritillaria meleagris *provides!*

Madonna lily

Lilium candidum

IF I COULD GROW only one lily (God forbid!), there's no doubt in my mind that it would be the Madonna lily. No other flower can boast a statelier habit, a purer shade of white, or a more delicious fragrance. Writing in 1931, Mrs. Grieve remarks in her *A Modern Herbal* that "it has been cultivated in this country for over three centuries, and no cottage garden was considered complete without this old favourite."

In fact, its history stretches much farther back in time than that. Most botanists now agree that the Madonna lily is native to the Balkans, although its widespread distribution in the wild makes this hypothesis difficult to confirm. Nevertheless it seems likely that the plant was brought to the Middle East by the Phoenicians and was then taken up by the Egyptians, the Greeks and the Romans, all of whom appear to have used it medicinally as well as for ornamentation. The Minoans (*c.* 1500 BC) also used it extensively for decoration, as their surviving frescoes and vases will attest.

It was the Romans (and not the Crusaders) who distributed the Madonna lily throughout Europe during their occupation, and this is when the plant first appeared in Britain. Indeed, Madonna lilies were so well known in England during the Middle Ages that the plant was considered a native species. For centuries these flowers have been equated with the Virgin Mary, but this is a relatively recent development. Bede the Venerable (673–735) was the first to single out the Madonna lily as a suitable flower to represent the Virgin — the white petals symbolizing the pureness of her body, and the golden anthers the pulchritude of her soul.

Madonna lilies are distinct from other lilies in several respects. In the first place, the bulbs should be planted shallowly, with the soil barely covering their growing point. Hardy to zone 5, in colder areas the bulbs may be planted more deeply, with a winter mulch to ensure additional protection.

Second, Madonna lilies go dormant after blooming in early summer and virtually disappear from the garden until early autumn when a rosette of fresh leaves appear that will overwinter, evergreen under the snow. In very early spring, many of these overwintering leaves will brown and shrivel, and new leaves will be produced from which the flowering spikes arise.

Lastly, unlike most members of its genera, Madonna lilies prefer alkaline soil, so if your native soil tends to be acidic, be sure to add some lime before planting. No matter what kind of soil you have, make certain that it's well-drained in the area where you intend to plant. It may be necessary to add some sand or crushed gravel in heavy clay soils to enhance drainage. Whatever you do, remember that these lilies resent domestic upheaval, so decide where they're to be planted, and then leave them alone. The best flowers are always produced by plants that have been "neglected" for decades.

The species name *candidum* doesn't just mean white, but "pure" or "dazzling" white, and this is absolutely appropriate. Even the superb white Regal lily (*L. regale*) can't hold a candle to the blinding white glossiness of the Madonna. Growing from 2.5 to 4 feet (75 to 120 centimeters) tall, this lily's blooms coincide with the flowering of the delphiniums in late June or early July, and the two plants seem natural companions. Anywhere from five to twenty flowers adorn each spike, and pale yellow pollen will often be seen cascading down the fragrant trumpets. Later in the summer, when the lilies have stopped showing off, self-seeded *Verbena bonariensis* transform the same area into a purple haze.

There are only two obstacles that stand between you and the successful cultivation of Madonna lilies. One is the fungal disease gray mold (*Botrytis elliptica*), to which these lilies are prone. As a precaution, it's a good idea to isolate Madonna lilies from other members of the *Lilium* genera, and to toss out any clumps that exhibit signs of infection. Early signs include spotting and blotching of the foliage. To determine if these symptoms are an indication of gray mold, place "diseased" plant parts under a bell jar where humid conditions prevail. If the disease is caused by *Botrytis*, gray mold will develop in several days on plant tissue. This isn't as great or common a problem as it used to be, since many of these lilies are now produced from virus-free stock, and are therefore free of disease, or "clean," to begin with. I have to admit that my own Madonnas reside in close proximity to a clump of trumpet lily hybrids, but I've never had a problem with either variety.

The second impediment to be overcome is that of limited bulb availability in a rather narrow time span. Madonna lilies don't last long out of the soil. Growers harvest the bulbs in late July (after flowering), and they are usually offered for sale at garden centers for just a few weeks at the end of August, at which time they will need to be planted pronto. This last prerequisite requires some consumer vigilance on your part, which may be exacerbated by the fact that at the end of August, most gardeners are feeling horticulturally pooped. To overcome this undeniable fact of life, some nurseries now allow you to place your lily order in the spring for special shipment as soon as the bulbs become available — without a doubt, the best method.

If this were a "scratch-n-sniff" book, this would be your favorite page! In addition to resplendent white flowers coupled with a majestic habit, Lilium candidum *possesses one of the most intoxicating fragrances you'll ever encounter. I like to combine it with the 'Round Table' delphinium series and alpine sea holly (*Eryngium alpinum*).*

Much of the scant hybridizing of Madonna lilies has concentrated on crossing them with other lily species to produce larger, colorful blooms. This seems to defeat the purpose of growing Madonna lilies in the first place, and I prefer the straight species. One strain that has been developed simply by selecting superior specimens of Madonna lilies and crossing them is the 'Cascade Strain' developed by George Slate at the Oregon Bulb Farm. These are handsome plants of great vigor, which are also much safer bets for our North American cottage gardens since they're grown from virus-free stock.

Remember what Mrs. Grieve said about Madonna lilies and cottage gardens: Keep the tradition alive and plant some of your own next August. William Blake (1757–1827) sums these plants up well when he writes:

> The modest rose puts forth a thorn,
> The humble sheep a threat'ning horn:
> While the Lily white shall in love delight,
> Nor a thorn nor a threat stain her beauty bright.

NAME: Madonna lily *Lilium candidum*
HEIGHT: 3 to 5' (1 to 1.5 m)
EXPOSURE: Sun
BLOOMING PERIOD: Summer
SOIL: Ordinary to rich garden soil with good drainage
COMPANIONS: Associates well with *Verbena bonariensis*, and for contrast and late season bloom, try planting some variegated sedum (*Sedum erythrostictum* 'Mediovariegatum') nearby
SPECIAL NOTES: Once planted, Madonna lilies should be left in place — they resent disturbance

The big three

WITHOUT A DOUBT, the bulk of any bulb order will consist primarily of "the big three" of the geophyte world: crocuses, daffodils and tulips. Certainly no cottage garden could be considered complete without them, and they are a vital and glorious source of springtime color. Crocuses should be planted near the house and beside walkways where they can be appreciated at close quarters. They also spread marvelously well in turfgrass, as do daffodils. Both are excellent candidates for naturalizing under deciduous shrubs and trees. Tulips tend to look more at home in the borders proper, and are to forget-me-nots what hollandaise is to asparagus.

In the world of geophytes, "antique" or "heirloom" bulb varieties are generally reckoned to be at least 50 years old, cutting in half the time it would take for a herbaceous perennial to acquire the same distinction. In addition to the eye-catching, newly hybridized cultivars, keep a look out for some of the older varieties — they have stood the test of time, and will make permanent, rather than fleeting additions to your cottage garden.

Larger spring bulbs (daffodils, tulips and hyacinths) can be over-planted with small bulbs for successional or simultaneous flowering. Here daffodils associate happily with the true-blue flowers of glory-of-the-snow (Chionodoxa spp.) Other small bulbs useful for over-planting include Crocus spp., squill (Scilla spp.), grape hyacinth (Muscari spp.), and Brimeura amethystina.

❧ Crocuses

After the arrival of the snowdrops and winter aconite, the next springtime flowers to appear are invariably those of the crocus. Most cottage gardeners will concentrate on the hybrids of just two species: the snow crocus (*C. chrysanthus*), and the giant Dutch crocus (*C. vernus*).

These cultivars are largely the handiwork of our old English friend E. A. Bowles in conjunction with the famous Dutch firm of van Tubergen, based in Haarlem, and most date from before World War I. Some celebrate the Dutch connection (for example, 'Zwanenburg Bronze'), while Bowles' selections tend to be named after birds ('Blue Bird', for example). Still widely available are:

C. CHRYSANTHUS CULTIVARS, HEIGHT 3"
'Advance' – Violet and yellow outside, peach interior
'Cream Beauty' – Cream yellow outside, dark yellow interior
'Prins Claus' – Purple blotch on white outside, pure white interior
'Snow Bunting' – Lilac feathering on white outside, yellow interior

C. VERNUS CULTIVARS, HEIGHT 4–5"
Surviving exceptionally well in turfgrass, these cultivars are the result of centuries of selection and subsequent propagation. Varieties with a Dickensian moniker usually indicate Victorian origins.
'King of the Whites'– White; also look for 'Queen of the Blues'
'Little Dorritt' – Silver gray, with a mauve blotch on the outside
'Pickwick' – Light blue background with purple venation
'Remembrance' – Deep violet

❧ Daffodils

Properly called Narcissus, daffodils are a huge genera divided into 10 divisions. Like the pansy tribe (*Viola* spp.), daffodils hybridize freely with one another. Start by trying a few from each of the following divisions, and allow the resulting plants to cohabit freely, à la Woodstock.

DIV. 1. TRUMPET DAFFODILS
'King Alfred', 18", Introduced 1890; golden yellow petals and trumpet
'Beersheba', 14", Introduced 1923; pure white petals and trumpet

DIV. 2. LARGE-CUPPED DAFFODILS
'Mrs. R. O. Blackhouse', 15", Introduced 1923; white petals, pink/apricot cup

DIV. 3. SMALL-CUPPED DAFFODILS
'Barrett Browning', 18", Introduced 1945; white petals, orange/red cup

DIV. 4. DOUBLE DAFFODILS
'Cheerfulness', 15", Introduced 1923; double white petals with cream center (also available is 'Yellow Cheerfulness')

DIV. 5. TRIANDUS HYBRID DAFFODILS
'Thalia', 16", Introduced 1916; 2 or more white blooms per stem with reflexed petals

DIV. 9. POETICUS DAFFODILS
'Actaea', 16", Introduced 1927; white petals with red-rimmed cup and orange eye

DIV. 10. WILD DAFFODILS AND NATURAL HYBRIDS
N. bulbocodium 'Conspicuous', 6–10", Introduced before 1850; yellow funnel-shaped flowers

∾ Tulips

It's useless to attempt resisting the allure of modern tulip cultivars, and indeed, they will enrich your garden tapestry immeasurably. Nevertheless, for sheer endurance and absolute charm, try to include some of the following old-fashioned varieties. I find that the newer cultivars (post-World War II) make excellent cut flowers, while antique varieties seem better suited to long-term tenancy in the herbaceous border. For added interest, include some clump-forming species tulips, many of which are hardy to zone 2. Like daffodils, tulips have been separated into "divisions" in an attempt to keep things organized. Although tulips are technically "old-fashioned" at 50 years of age, I try to enforce a slightly stricter criterion, and only consider pre-World War I cultivars as genuinely heirloom.

DIV. 1. SINGLE EARLY TULIPA CULTIVARS
'Diana', 12" (30 cm), Introduced 1909; large ivory blooms on strong stems
'Pink Beauty', 12" (30 cm), Introduced 1889; electric pink with a white edge
'Prince of Austria', 16" (40 cm), Introduced 1860; brick red with a yellow base, fragrant
'Van der Neer', 10" (25 cm), Introduced 1860; plum purple, occasionally 'breaks' to produce white feathering

DIV. 2. DOUBLE EARLY TULIPA CULTIVARS
'El Toreador', 10" (25 cm), Introduced 1890; orange streaked with deeper orange
'Murillo', 10" (25 cm), Introduced 1860; white flushed with pink, fragrant
'Scarlet Cardinal', 10" (25 cm), Introduced 1914; vivid scarlet, flushed with orange
'Schoonoord', 10" (25 cm), Introduced 1909; large pure white blooms; perfect with grape hyacinths (*Muscari* spp.)

DIV. 3. TRIUMPH TULIPA CULTIVARS
'Carrara', 22" (55 cm) Introduced 1912; big white petals, reminiscent of a water lily
'Couleur Cardinale', 14" (35 cm), Introduced 1845; large, cardinal-red weather-resistant blooms (sometimes classed as a Division I tulip)

DIV. 5. SINGLE LATE TULIPA CULTIVARS
'Clara Butt', 22" (55 cm), Introduced 1889; bright salmon pink, the most widely-grown tulip at the turn of the last century
'Greuze', 22" (55 cm), Introduced 1905; large, cup-shaped violet-purple flowers
'Philippe de Comines', 22" (55 cm), Introduced 1905; maroon black flowers
'Zomerschoon', 16" (40 cm), Introduced 1620; cream, feathered with pink flowers. Perhaps the oldest tulip still in cultivation along with 'Gala Beauty'

DIV. 9. REMBRANDT TULIPA CULTIVAR
'Gala Beauty', 24" (60 cm), Introduced 1620; yellow streaked with crimson. Formerly listed as 'Columbus' or 'French Crown'

DIV. 10. PARROT TULIPA CULTIVAR
'Fantasy', 22" (55 cm), Introduced 1910; huge, blowsy rose petals striped with green. Much fun!

CHAPTER SIX

Herbs

HERBS HAVE BEEN CULTIVATED for millennia and, as we've already discussed, were largely responsible for the advent of cottage gardens as we've come to understand them. Herbs were always planted near dwellings since they were used on such a regular basis, and gardens became medicine chests, spice racks and air freshener sources. Clearly, such important plants needed to be close at hand.

Many of the traditional herbs were used for strewing on the floors of cottages both to discourage insect pests (rue, tansy, wormwood) and also to freshen the air in these damp, musty lodgings (lavender, mint and sweet woodruff). Still other herbs were used to cure a multitude of physical complaints before the days when medicinal preparations were as close as the nearest drugstore. The most widespread use of these plants, however, both then and now, was in the kitchen. Spices were imported from the East, but for the most part they were well beyond the means of cottagers, who instead used the plants at hand to flavor their food. Many people think of "English cooking" and "bland" as synonymous, but they would be surprised to learn how wide and varied the palate of the average cottager was. As the Simon and Garfunkel song suggests, "parsley, sage, rosemary and thyme" formed the backbone of the culinary arsenal (notice that all are evergreen in most of England), but certainly, this was just the tip of the herbal iceberg.

The concept of a separate herb garden, isolated from other flowering plants, would have been inconceivable to cottage gardeners.

Segregating herbs from other flowering plants would have been unthinkable to early cottage gardeners, so be sure to include as many as you can in your overall design. Some of the oldest cottage garden herbs such as borage (Borago officinalis, pictured here) hail from the Mediterranean region and are therefore perfect for hot, droughty conditions.

Everything grew together, and it's unlikely that herbs proper would even have been considered as distinct from the other plants in the cottage borders. The first herbs to inhabit the cottage garden were mostly of Mediterranean origin, having been brought to Britain by the Romans. These plants usually make their homes on the dry rocky ledges of the Mediterranean region, in areas where the sun beats down on them day after day, and it's a good idea to remember this when positioning herbs in your garden. Ordinary garden soil is fine for most herbs — in fact, very rich soil isn't desirable as it may result in excessive lush, green growth. Good drainage is important, as is a full-sun location. The flavor of herbs is intensified by the oils that collect in the plant tissue to protect it from the burning rays of the sun. For instance, basil grown in partly shaded conditions will have a fraction of the flavor of a plant grown in full sun.

Borage

❧

Borago officinalis

BORAGE IS A COTTAGE garden plant *par excellence* and has been grown in Britain since Roman times. A hardy, self-seeding annual, this plant is nothing if not carefree, sporting bright blue or white edible flowers. Native to the Mediterranean region, borage is closely related to comfrey (*Symphytum officinale*). Both species have hairy leaves and a taste and odor reminiscent of cucumber.

Once established, borage will spread pleasingly around the garden. Growing about 24 inches high (60 centimeters) with a spread of 18 inches (45 centimeters), its large black seeds should be directly sown in the open ground in early spring for midsummer blooms, which will continue to be produced until the first hard frosts. Borage is especially useful for maintaining blue shades in the late-summer garden as the golden-hued flowers begin to make their presence increasingly felt. Often planted adjacent to apiaries, the high nectar content of the flowers ensure that plenty of honeybees will visit your garden, and explains the old country name for the plant, "bee-bread."

There's some debate as to how borage acquired its name, but for centuries it has been connected with courage. In medieval times, borage flowers were embroidered on the scarves of warriors to give them courage and strength in battle, and it was traditional for jousters to drink borage tea prior to tournaments. One possibility is that the Latin *borago* is a corruption of "corago" (*cor* meaning "heart," and *ago*, "I bring"). Equally plausible is the suggestion that the name is derived from the Celtic *borrach*, or "man of courage." The idea that borage brought courage may be due in part to the fact that the flowers were often used as a garnish for wine cups and were thought to intensify the alcoholic effect of the drink. This notion isn't as quaint as we might imagine. After all, who hasn't heard the expression "Dutch courage" in our own time, which certainly alludes to the same concept.

Even if borage wasn't edible, I'd grow lots of it anyway for its ornamental star-shaped flowers and prominent black anthers. All parts of the plant are edible, but if you decide to give the hirsute leaves a try, go for the very youngest ones, and chop them up finely. Personally, I prefer to stick to the flowers. In addition to their well-known use as a garnish for claret cup and Pimm's No. 1 cocktails, they look terrific added to salads or cottage cheese, where they will subtly impart their delicate cucumber flavor. The flowers are also frequently used in ice cubes, but be sure to use distilled water to prevent the cubes from clouding. Candied borage and violet flowers add a refined touch to cakes and pastries. In other recipes where parsley is used as a garnish, try substituting borage flowers. Martha Stewart would approve, I'm sure!

Borage was used in herbal medicine for centuries to treat fever, kidney complaints and bronchial infections. Borage poultices were applied to the skin to relieve rheumatism and skin disorders. In modern medicine, borage may be poised to make a comeback. This is because its seeds contain gamma-linolenic acid (GLA), one of the fatty acids essential to humans for the maintenance of cell functions. Gamma-linolenic acid is currently being explored as a treatment for premenstrual syndrome, diabetes and alcoholism, as well as showing some therapeutic promise for the prevention of strokes and heart disease. High levels of GLA are present in human milk and are thought to be important for the development of brain tissue in infants. As much as 15 percent of the general population may suffer from depressed GLA levels, and research into using GLA as a dietary supplement for these people is ongoing.

Borage isn't the only plant to contain GLA in its seeds. Marijuana (*Cannabis sativa*), currants (*Ribes* spp.) and evening primrose (*Oenothera biennis*) seeds all contain the acid, although not in such high quantities. The green parts of borage also contain low levels of pyrrolizidine alkaloids which are thought to cause liver damage, although it's unlikely to be a problem unless you begin grazing on a bushel or two every morning with your coffee. It's important to remember that any plant can be detrimental

A classic cottage garden herb, borage (Borago officinalis) bears star-shaped edible blue flowers with a light cucumber flavor. It's the traditional adornment to Pimm's cocktails and claret cup, but don't forget to add borage blossoms to summer salads or use them instead of chopped parsley to garnish entrees.

to human health if ingested in large quantities. Comfrey contains much higher levels of pyrrolizidine than borage does, which is why its use as a herbal remedy has recently been banned in some countries.

Several obstacles stand in the way of borage being exploited as a commercial source of GLA. Principal among these is the fact that borage plants flower over a long season and are constantly producing

NAME: Borage *Borago officinalis*
HEIGHT: To 2' (60 cm)
EXPOSURE: Sun
BLOOMING PERIOD: Summer to autumn
SOIL: Ordinary to poor garden soil
COMPANIONS: Looks great with other plants that also bear edible flowers such as nasturtium (*Tropaeolum majus*) and pot marigold (*Calendula officinalis*)
SPECIAL NOTES: Self-seeds easily. Keep an eye out for the white-flowered variety

seeds. Since all the seeds don't ripen at the same time, harvesting them becomes time-consuming and expensive. In addition, borage seeds are scattered far and wide as soon as they reach maturity, making their collection even more complicated. Finally, farmers who practice crop rotation may not look kindly on borage as its seeds remain viable for up to eight years, guaranteeing plenty of volunteer plants for several seasons after the initial sowing. While these inclinations may frustrate farmers, they add up to a plant with the perfect personality for the North American cottage garden.

Although the blue-flowered form of borage is by far the most common, don't overlook the white form which is just as appealing and is usually sold as *Borago officinalis* 'Alba'. I always try to plant both colors together. There are also some rose-colored cultivars around, but I find the color somewhat insipid compared to the blue and white types. I have also read (but never seen it) that a borage cultivar exists with variegated leaves, but I think it unlikely that this would come true from seed. No matter — it would be a case of gilding the lily in any event.

The next time you're feeling timid or depressed, why not amble out to the garden and pick some borage? After all, as Robert Burton (1577–1640) wrote in his *Anatomy of Melancholy* (1621):

> Borage and Hellebore fill two scenes
> Sovereign plants to purge the veins
> Of melancholy, and cheer the heart
> Of those black fumes which make it smart.

Fennel

Foeniculum vulgare

FENNEL IS ONE of the most beautiful and statuesque herbs that you can possibly grow, and no North American cottage garden should be without it. Hardy to zone 5 or 6, in colder areas it should be grown as a hardy annual. In addition to the usual green variety, I always grow bronze fennel. There is a certain amount of dispute over what this should be correctly called, botanically speaking, but suffice to say it will be listed as either *F. vulgare* 'Bronze' or *F. vulgare* 'Purpureum', and you'll know it when you see it. The bronze cultivars also appear to be more winter-hardy than the green types.

The intricately dissected leaves are graceful and feathery up close, and from a distance the substantial 4- to 5-foot (1.2 to 1.5 m) plants make a dramatic statement. A member of the Umbelliferae or parsley family, fennel was used by the ancient Egyptians both medicinally and for food. Native to the Mediterranean, it was brought to Britain by the Romans who used it to flavor meat. Later, Charlemagne (742–814) insisted that it be grown in great

Perilla grows 2 to 3 feet (60 to 90 centimeters) tall in ordinary garden soil, although if you grow it in rich soil you will get considerably more foliage. If this is the case, be sure to pinch back the growing tips of the plant to encourage a bushier habit. Perilla grows well in full sun to part shade, and while virtually a disease-free plant, in some seasons snails and slugs may prove to be a nuisance.

It's easy to start perilla from seed outdoors. Seed should be sprinkled on the soil surface (it needs light to germinate) in early autumn as the seeds require a chilling period outdoors over the winter months. In nature, perilla begins flowering as the days become shorter, signaling that summer is drawing to a close. Plants whose flowering period is triggered by the length of daylight they receive (for example, chrysanthemums and poinsettias) are known as photo-sensitive. In the autumn, perilla leaves will drop at the first frost, but don't despair, they'll be back next year!

Several cultivars of perilla are available, and if you're after one of these, it's probably much easier to buy a few plants from your garden center in the spring, or beg them from a gardening friend who will probably be only too glad to pass some along. Perilla has been listed in American seed catalogs since at least 1891, but many gardeners are still oblivious to its existence, which is a shame.

My first perilla plants came from a fellow horticulturist who grows the old-fashioned 'Bronze' type. This is an interesting combination of green and purple together, which as you may have guessed looks bronze from a distance. The solid purple form of perilla is offered as *P. frutescens* 'Atropurpurea' and makes a very good garden subject, but the superior cultivar to my eye is the frilly-margined deep purple *P. frutescens* 'Crispa', a really lovely plant by anybody's standards. While it's true that perilla will never be the star of your garden, it plays an important supporting role, and as every thespian knows, a true star requires a reliable chorus.

Perilla, like all herbs, should be consumed in moderation. Recently, there have been concerns over one of the compounds found in the plant called "perilla ketone." The concentration of perilla ketone increases during flowering and fruiting. Described as a potent lung toxin, it can cause respiratory distress and has been implicated in cattle poisoning after ruminants have grazed on large quantities of the plant.

Experts agree that different types of perilla show considerable chemical diversity, so while one plant might be harmful, its neighbor may be benign. If you're given to culinary Russian roulette, here's a helpful hint. Perilla suitable for human consumption generally has a mild, agreeable fragrance, while perilla with a strong or unpleasant fragrance may be harmful. Only your nose knows for sure!

NAME: Perilla *Perilla frutescens*
HEIGHT: 2 to 3' (60 to 90 cm)
EXPOSURE: Sun to part shade
BLOOMING PERIOD: Late summer
SOIL: Ordinary garden soil
COMPANIONS: The foliage of purple perilla is useful for setting off some of the deeper colored bergamots (*Monarda didyma*) or for subduing the brighter shades of Jerusalem cross (*Lychnis chalcedonica*)
SPECIAL NOTES: Self-seeds easily, although some springtime thinning may be required

More Herbs for the Cottage Garden

IN ADDITION TO the herbs we've examined up close, there is a plenitude of other marvelous plants well-suited to the North American cottage garden. Here are 20 suggestions for filling in the nooks and crannies that these plants love. With the exception of chives and mint, all of the following herbs prefer a full-sun location.

Lemon balm (*Melissa officinalis*). Perennial herb, hardy to zones 3 to 4. The genus name *Melissa*, Greek for "bee," is apt, since this plant's essential oil gives off an odor very reminiscent of honeybee pheromone (a chemical sexual attractant). Needless to say, this induces bees of all kinds to swarm the plant, especially when in flower, so don't plant it too close to your house. Lemon balm leaves are a good substitute for recipes calling for lemon thyme (*Thymus x citriodorus*). Leaves may also be used in salads, soups and stuffings, or in fish and vegetable dishes. Growing lemon balm on lean or dry soils will discourage its naturally rambunctious disposition.

Basil (*Ocimum basilicum*). Tender annual. I consider basil essential for fresh tomato dishes, but its other uses in the kitchen seem endless. Available in several flavors (Anise, Lemon, Licorice, Spicey Globe) and a variety of leaf shapes and colors (Dark Opal, Large Leaf, Lettuce Leaf, Purple Ruffles). Unlike most herbs, basil grows best in fairly rich soil.

Bergamot (*Monarda* spp. and cultivars). Perennial to zone 4. Also known as beebalm and Oswego tea — not surprisingly since bergamot is responsible for the distinctive taste of Earl Grey tea. Look for mildew-resistant cultivars.

Betony (*Stachys officinalis*). Producing rose or white flowers in midsummer, betony is a perennial herb, 1 to 2 feet (30 to 60 centimeters) high, and hardy to zone 5. Betony was once considered a medical panacea for a variety of maladies, but its use nowadays is principally restricted to herbal teas and as a garden ornamental.

Salad Burnet (*Sanguisorba minor* subsp. *minor*). A long-lived, vigorous perennial plant, hardy to zones 3 to 4, salad burnet is a member of the rose family. Cultivated since ancient times first as a medicinal plant, and then as a food source, salad burnet was brought to the New World by early European colonists. Tolerant of most soil types, fresh young leaves are an excellent addition to spring salads where they impart a delicate cucumber flavor, which is complemented admirably by a rich creamy dressing. Also excellent with most fish as well as a delicious addition to herbal vinaigrettes or incorporated into cream cheese. After flowering, cut plants back to within 2 inches (5 centimeters) of the soil surface for a fresh crop several weeks later.

German Chamomile (*Matricaria recutita*). A sweet-scented annual, German chamomile is capable of growing as high as 3 feet (1 meter), given ideal conditions. Widely used in tea, an estimated 1 million cups per day are consumed worldwide. What many people are unaware of is that German chamomile is closely related to ragweed, and people allergic to this weed may also experience an allergic response from German chamomile preparations. Easily grown from seed, German chamomile is sometimes confused with Roman chamomile (*Chamaemelum nobile*) which is perennial to at least zone 5. Roman chamomile was also used as a sedative or tonic, but is best remembered for its use as a substitute for turfgrass in Elizabethan England. Both types thrive in full sun and average garden soil.

Chervil (*Anthriscus cerefolium*). Chervil is an annual plant, native to Eurasia, with sweet-smelling white flowers, resembling those of Queen Anne's lace. First used as a culinary herb by the ancient Syrians, modern cooks still prize the delicate young leaves, which impart a subtle pepper and licorice flavor to such classic French sauces as béchamel and ravigote, without which life would hardly be worth living. Unlike most herbs, chervil is happiest in partly shaded conditions and prefers a rich, well-drained soil. It is intolerant of prolonged heat waves.

Chives (*Allium schoenoprasum*). Perennial to zones 3 to 4. Chives impart a delicate onion flavor and are widely used raw in spring salads or with cream cheese, chopped over baked potatoes with sour cream, or cooked in soups, sauces, eggs or fish. A completely care-free plant, chives bear attractive pale purple flowers in early summer.

Comfrey (*Symphytum officinale* and cultivars). Perennial to zones 3 to 4. The foliage of this plant is considered a compost additive *par excellence* as it is very rich in nitrogen, phosphorus, potassium and calcium. Fresh foliage steeped for a week in water can be used

Low-growing fragrant herbs like lavender and thyme are perfect plants for filling in around flagstone pathways where their scent can be appreciated "up close and personal." Although they tend to look somewhat scruffy after the snows melt, these herbs will respond well to a springtime trim.

as a rich (if smelly) "manure tea" especially good for New World vegetables like tomatoes, cucumbers and squash. No longer recommended for human consumption.

Dill (*Anethum graveolens*). An annual plant, usually growing about 20 inches (50 centimeters) tall, and bearing small yellow flowers. Dill is one of the oldest documented herbs, having been mentioned in an Egyptian list of medicinals over 5,000 years ago. But it wasn't exploited commercially in North America until the early 1800s. Essential in pickled vegetables (and cucumbers in particular), dill has a plethora of other uses in the kitchen from salads to seafood, and poultry to dressings and sauces. Like chervil, dill should be added to cooked dishes at the last minute, as its flavor is reduced with long exposure to heat. Dill is a cool-season crop and should be sown in early spring for early to midsummer harvest. In most parts of North America, dill is a reliable self-seeder.

Lavender (*Lavandula angustifolia*). Perennial to zones 5 to 6. Lavender looks as good as it smells, and if it's hardy in your area (the cultivar 'Munstead' seems to be the best in colder zones), you would be remiss not to include it. Although it has many uses, I still love it best casually strewn throughout a chest of drawers. Prefers poor soil on the dry side.

Licorice (*Glycyrrhiza glabra*). Cultivated since classical Greek times, licorice is a perennial legume (capable of fixing atmospheric nitrogen), hardy to zones 5 to 6. Brought to the New World by early English settlers, it was quickly adopted by native Americans as a medicinal herb and is still an important ingredient in modern pharmaceuticals, including cough and cold preparations as well as laxatives. Most of us know it best in its role as a delicious confection. Deep, moisture-retentive soil will furnish the right conditions for optimum root and rhizome growth (the delicious bits), and a full sun location will encourage lush leafy growth complemented by pinky-violet flowers in midsummer. Decidedly ornamental and much underrated.

Parsley (*Petroselinum crispum* and cultivars). Biennial to zones 5 to 6. Used extensively as a throw-away garnish in the past, parsley is being re-embraced as a useful addition to sauces, dressings, eggs, shellfish, fish and meat dishes. An essential ingredient in tabouleh. Available in a plain-leaved form (Dark Green Italian, Paramount) or curled-leaved form (Afro, Champion Moss Curled, Exotica, Sherwood, Unicurl).

Rosemary (*Rosmarinus officinalis* and cultivars). Perennial to zones 7 to 8. Just consult any cookbook, and you'll be amazed how many dishes call for rosemary, although it's most commonly used in recipes containing lamb. In the Mediterranean where rosemary grows wild, its fragrance becomes so intense that when the wind is right, it can be smelled 20 miles (37 kilometers) out to sea.

Sage (*Salvia officinalis* and cultivars). Perennial to zones 5 to 6. The leaves of sage are used in soups, stews, pork, duck and sausage dishes, and especially poultry stuffing. Bearing beautiful sky-blue flowers in early summer, sage is said to thrive only "where the wife rules." Cultivars such as 'Icterina', 'Purpurascens' and 'Tricolor' are less hardy than the species.

Winter Savory (*Satureja montana*). A hardy perennial dwarf sub-shrub, hardy to zones 4 to 5. Closely related to the annual summer savory (*S. hortensis*), the peppery tang of winter savory is often considered inferior to that of summer savory. In France, winter savory is recommended for fresh trout; in Italy, it is used in the manufacture of vermouth. I find it a useful addition to fish, poultry and soups. Growing well in poor soils, winter savory is drought tolerant and sufficiently upright in habit to perform the function of a casual low hedge, with the added bonus of tiny pink flowers reminiscent of heather (*Calluna vulgaris*). Several cultivars are available, including 'Nana' and 'Prostrate White'.

Sorrel (*Rumex acetosa* and cultivars). Perennial to zone 3. Although native to Eurasia, it has become naturalized across North America as far north as Alaska. In the mid-1800s, native Americans living along the Colorado River used the seeds as a source of flour. Raw leaves can be added to salad, where they impart a slightly sour tang, or cooked in sauces, or best of all, classic sorrel soup. The stronger flavored French sorrel (*R. scutatus*) is the preferred variety in Europe.

Spearmint (*Mentha spicata*). Perennial to zones 3 to 4. Having invasive tendencies, spearmint is best grown in a container or in a semi-wild setting — don't let it loose in your borders! More useful than peppermint (*M. x piperita*) in the kitchen, spearmint is the consummate choice for garnishing lamb, making mint sauce or jelly, or boiling with green peas — not to mention that Kentucky favorite: mint juleps!

❧Tarragon (*Artemisia dracunculus*). Perennial to zone 4, and native to both Eurasia and western North America. Avoid 'Russian' tarragon which will self-seed, whereas the superior French tarragon can only be propagated by division. Tarragon has a multitude of uses in the kitchen, especially in French cuisine, but even if it wasn't good for anything else, I'd treasure it as the secret ingredient in real Dijon mustard, and of course, for what it does to béarnaise sauce!

*The symbol of happiness, fidelity and love, rosemary (*Rosmarinus officinalis*) has been included in European wedding bouquets for the past 1,000 years. Hardy to zones 7 to 8, the plant is slow growing initially, but once established, its roots sink deep into the soil making it extremely drought tolerant.*

Thyme (*Thymus vulgaris*). Perennial, hardiness varies. The thymes comprise a large family of plants — some are grown for their flavor (lemon thyme, caraway thyme), others are grown for their decorative foliage (silver thyme), and still others for their flowers (Mother-of-thyme). While its culinary uses are legion, Carl Linnaeus (1701–78), the father of modern botanical nomenclature, recommended thyme as a cure for hangovers!

CHAPTER SEVEN

Vegetables

IT WILL DEPEND ON your individual taste as to whether you decide to grow a lot of vegetables or just a few. For the early cottagers, growing vegetables and herbs was a matter of life or death and often made the difference between surviving the winter or dying of starvation. Self-sufficiency was a necessity. Fortunately, modern cottagers don't have to endure these constraints, but few would argue that homegrown produce tastes better than store bought, and this is largely due to the fact that no supermarket will be able to compete with you when it comes to freshness.

The next decision will be where to plant the produce. I would urge you to forgo the modern concept of planting out in straight rows, or even worse, grouping all the vegetables together in one section of the garden. It wasn't until relatively recently that farmers began planting their crops in rows. The appropriately named "Turnip" Townsend invented the horse-drawn seed drill, and while this was a very efficient method of seeding large areas, it brought with it straight lines, and the pest and disease problems we now associate with monoculture farming. Up until the early 1700s, cottagers and farmers alike grew vegetables in small patches along with the flowers and fruit, and invariably practiced crop rotation. This, then, is the Right Approach.

It doesn't take a practiced eye to see how well vegetables, herbs and flowers blend together in this archetypal cottage garden scenario. Rotating crops and resisting the urge to plant vegetables in straight rows will go a long way toward minimizing potential insect and disease problems.

Vegetables can be grown in the spaces left by spring-flowering bulbs or can be rotated with annual flowers. Adding compost or composted manure for plants that produce their crop above the ground is important. These crops can then be followed with the lighter-feeding root vegetables without any further soil amendments. Before you know it, your vegetables will be dancing a slow tango all over your cottage garden.

Most cottage gardeners will want to start some of their vegetables from seed, and luckily for you, vegetables are among the easiest plants to sprout. Growing from seed will also enable you to grow some of the old heirloom varieties, which often aren't available as seedlings at garden centers. Some cottage gardeners will choose to cultivate modern varieties, while others will want to grow exclusively old-fashioned ones. If you're just starting out, it's a good idea to include some recent cultivars since these are usually the most disease and pest resistant. I well remember one year when I was growing only heirloom tomatoes, all of which were susceptible to tobacco mosaic virus, a serious disease of the Solanaceae (nightshade family). It only took one visit from a smoker to effectively wipe out the crop. As you get more adept at vegetable gardening, you can easily add increasing numbers of the older varieties.

Taking tomatoes as an example, it's easy to see the difference between old and new varieties. Tomatoes bred for large-scale modern cultivation will possess two important characteristics that heirloom varieties lack. First, they will tend to set one large crop that ripens all at the same time. This is fine if you plan to send your produce to market and want to harvest your crop only once. But what home gardener wants all their tomatoes to ripen in the space of one week? Clearly, staggered ripening dates suit most home gardeners best, and even then there are times of the year when seasonal gluts mean that even your neighbors and friends will get tired of your munificent contributions.

Secondly, large-scale operations generally need to ship their produce a considerable distance from where it was grown, and to survive the jostling, tomatoes must have thick skins. Again, this amounts to more of a minus than a plus for cottage gardeners. Who wants to bite into a tomato with a reptilian hide?

So why else should you aspire to the cultivation of heirloom varieties? Broadly speaking, because if we don't grow them, they will very likely become obsolete. Vegetables remain vegetables only because humans re-plant them year after year. This characteristic becomes a potential problem when old varieties become extinct, and breeders need fresh genetic material to create new varieties. There is also no question but that many of the old varieties have a superior flavor that has been forfeited for uniformity of size, color, ripening time, shipping durability, and a multitude of other traits that cottage gardeners needn't be concerned with.

Most exciting of all, there's a good chance that when you grow an heirloom variety, you'll relish a flavor that no one else in your family has experienced for 200 years, so go ahead and spoil yourself. While you're at it, don't feel obliged to grow only those vegetables with which you are familiar. Our forebears may have eaten vegetables only when they were in season, but they certainly enjoyed a wider variety of produce than we do. In addition to the old standbys, try enlarging your palate with some "antique" produce such as cardoons, salsify and scorzonera.

Cardoon

Cynara cardunculus

YOU MAY BE forgiven if you've never heard of cardoon before, but in fact, it was one of the very first vegetable plants to be used as food by humans and was already considered "ancient" when the Greeks and Romans cultivated it. A member of the Compositae or daisy family and native to the Mediterranean region, cardoon is closely related to the globe artichoke (*Cynara scolymus*) and is perennial to zone 7. In most areas, however, it is grown as an annual vegetable.

It is the leafstalk or main rib which is eaten, the green leafy parts of the plant being extremely bitter. When trimmed and washed, the stalks look like large celery sticks. Even if you aren't interested in cardoon as a vegetable, it makes an outstanding ornamental. Graham Stuart Thomas calls it "the grandest of all silverlings." Capable of growing as high as 4 to 5 feet (1.2 to 1.5 meters) in a single season, cardoons are blessed with some of the most beautiful foliage of any plant you'll ever grow — feather-shaped gray-green leaves with deep curves and covered with fine white down. By late summer, some varieties will produce large mauve flower heads that resemble thistles.

There are two kinds of cardoon, known as Spanish and French (or Tours). The Spanish variety is preferable as the leaves are free of spines and therefore easier to handle. It is also less likely to produce flowers, which many gardeners are inclined to remove anyway (they make excellent cut flowers). The French type tends to have spines on the ends of its leaves, much like a thistle, and generally has a slightly coarser appearance. Named cultivars include 'Italian Dwarf' and 'Plein Blanc Enorme'. Cardoon was first recorded growing in cottage gardens in 1658, but there's little question that it was cultivated extensively before this date.

Cardoon seeds should be started indoors several weeks before the last frost date for your area. Seeds sprout easily and quickly. Young seedlings may be planted out when all danger of frost is past and should be spaced 2 to 3 feet (60 to 90 centimeters) apart. Cardoons prefer full sun and rich soil, and ample moisture is important if they are to be consumed. Lack of water during the growing season can lead to hollow, stringy stems which will render the cardoons inedible. Cardoons are usually blanched before harvest. Blanching is the process whereby light is withheld from the plants in order that green tissue which would normally continue to photosynthesize becomes white. Blanching also makes the stems more tender and increases sugars in the blanched areas.

The blanching process should begin two to three weeks before the expected harvest date (mid-autumn). After making sure that the leaves are dry (or they'll rot), they should be gathered up from their base and held together in a loosely conical shape. Once they are in a vertical position, wrap cardboard around the plant from soil level to within several inches (centimeters) of the leaf tips, with just a few of the top leaves spilling out. Secure the cardboard cones with string or tape, and you may need to add a stake to keep the whole structure in place. This system is much less labor-intensive than the alternative, which is to grow cardoons in trenches, gradually hilling the soil up over them, which produces the same blanched leafstalks.

I have also seen cardoon used as a fast-growing annual hedge, and when grown like this they look

Being both edible and highly ornamental, cardoon (Cynara cardunculus) is without a doubt one of the most neglected of cottage garden plants. Requiring rich, moist soil in a sunny location, cardoon plants often attain heights of 5 feet (1.5 meters) or more. It's perennial only to zones 7 to 8, so gardeners in colder areas should sow seed indoors several weeks before the last frost date, to be transplanted outside once the ground has warmed up.

Cardoon Combo

1 medium-sized cardoon, trimmed and cut into
   1- to 2-inch (2.5 to 5 cm) segments
2 tbsp. (30 mL) white vinegar or lemon juice
1 clove elephant garlic, minced
2 small onions, peeled and chopped
2 tbsp. (30 mL) virgin olive oil
3 Italian paste (Roma) tomatoes, sliced
thyme, oregano, salt and pepper to taste

Using a vegetable peeler, remove any tough outer strings
from the cardoon stalks.

Cook cardoon in boiling salted water with a little lemon juice
or vinegar (to prevent discoloring) for about 30 minutes, or
until tender. Drain.

Sauté garlic and onions in olive oil. Add tomatoes.
Simmer for 5 minutes, then add the cardoon.
Simmer for 5 more minutes and add seasoning. Serve.
Makes a great vegetable side-dish!

Serves 4–6

Golden Fried Cardoon

2 quarts (2 L) water
2 tbsp. (30 mL) white vinegar or lemon juice
4 large cardoon stalks, (about 1 lb./450 g) trimmed and
   cut into 2-inch (15 cm) segments
2 large eggs
1 cup (250 mL) breadcrumbs
¼ cup (60 mL) grated Parmesan cheese
½ tsp. (2 mL) salt
⅛ tsp. (1 mL) pepper
vegetable oil (for frying)
lemon wedges

Using a vegetable peeler, remove any tough outer strings
from the cardoon stalks.

Cook cardoon in boiling salted water with a little lemon juice
or vinegar (to prevent discoloring) for about 30 minutes, or
until tender. Drain.

Beat eggs in a shallow bowl. In another bowl, toss breadcrumbs and Parmesan with the salt and pepper. Dip the
cardoon in the egg, and then dredge it in the crumbs, press-
ing as required to be sure the breadcrumbs adhere. Set pieces
on a wax paper–lined tray.

In a medium skillet, heat ½ inch (1.25 cm) of vegetable oil
over moderately high heat. When the oil is hot, add the
cardoon, 5 to 6 pieces at a time, and fry until golden brown
(about 90 seconds per side). Drain excess oil (a wire rack over
a baking sheet works well). Sprinkle lightly with salt, and serve
with lemon wedges.

Serves 6

very regal. Cottage gardeners should be forewarned, however, that no matter where they grow their cardoons, they're sure to elicit the attention of neighbors. The standard form of query appears to be "What's *that*?" Watch for widening eyes as you explain it's "just an old vegetable."

Although cardoon is still rather rare in North America, it's fairly well known in Europe. The Italians call it *cardoni*, and I've seen it for sale at local markets in the autumn on both sides of the continent.

It would be unchivalrous to sing the praises of cardoon without making a few serving suggestions. If you're curious as to how the Victorians prepared cardoon, have a look at *Mrs. Beeton's*. It's hardly surprising that she recommends boiling them in water and then serving them with heaps of the ubiquitous white sauce. I think we can do better than that.

NAME: Cardoon *Cynara cardunculus*

HEIGHT: To 5' (1.5 m)

EXPOSURE: Sun

BLOOMING PERIOD: Late summer

SOIL: Rich garden soil

COMPANIONS: Terrific by itself or with other plants that will successfully vie for attention such as love-lies-bleeding (*Amaranthus caudatus*) or ornamental Chinese rhubarb (*Rheum palmatum* 'Atrosanguinium')

SPECIAL NOTES: Plants intended for the kitchen may be blanched before use

---

Salsify

Tragopogon porrifolius

SALSIFY IS ANOTHER ornamental vegetable that's easy to grow and, once established, will readily self seed around the cottage garden. This biennial is also known as oyster plant or vegetable oyster (although it doesn't taste a bit like oysters!), as well as purple goat's beard. It is closely related to yellow goat's beard (*Tragopogon dubius*), a weed common to both North America and Europe, which is called Jack-go-to-bed-at-noon in Britain due to its habit (like salsify) of closing its flowers at midday. The purple flowers arising from elegant grassy leaves are sufficiently ornamental that I grew salsify for several years in the herbaceous border before I ever tasted it.

The botanical name *Tragopogon* is from the Greek *tragos*, meaning "goat," and *pogon* meaning "a beard," a good example of a scientific name being directly translated into a common one, a fairly rare occurrence in the confusing world of botanical nomenclature. The species name of *porrifolius* means "with leaves like a leek" and is derived from the Latin *porrum*, or "leek." In spite of being native to the Mediterranean region, salsify is hardy to zone 4. *T. porrifolius* was known to the ancient Greeks and Romans, but rather than being cultivated in gardens, it was traditionally gathered wild. Indeed, there is very little difference between wild forms of salsify and named cultivars such as 'Mammoth Sandwich Island', first introduced in the 1860s and still the most widely grown.

By the fifteenth century, salsify had migrated from Italy to both France and Germany, and by

1656 it was certainly known in England, since it appears in a plant list of John Tradescant the Younger (1608–62). Whether he grew it as an ornamental or a vegetable is uncertain, but during the latter half of the seventeenth century it was imported to North America for both its nutritional and diuretic properties.

The young leaves of salsify as well as the unopened flower buds are edible, but it is for the long white taproot (similar in appearance to a parsnip) that salsify is grown. If you are growing salsify principally as a vegetable, you must be sure that the soil is free of stones, and that it hasn't been manured recently, otherwise the roots will become forked and misshapen. Sandy loam with a slightly alkaline pH will produce the best crops.

Salsify seeds don't have a very long shelf life and usually remain viable for only a year or two. The easiest way to start them off is to place the seeds between moist paper towels. In several days, a green tip (the radicle, or embryonic root) will emerge. As soon as this occurs, the seeds should be transferred to small pots filled with a sterile soilless mix until leaves appear. They can then be hardened off and transplanted into the open soil before their developing taproots become too large.

During the first year, you may get a few purple blooms, but in the second year all plants will flower and then develop seedheads that look like overgrown dandelion seed spheres. While salsify isn't as invasive as its next of kin, yellow goat's beard, it will produce sufficient numbers of seedlings for the next year's crop with a few extras left over to pass along to friends. If you're growing salsify primarily as an ornamental, deadheading second-year plants will extend your season of bloom considerably. Just

～ Cream of Salsify Soup

1 lb. (450 g) salsify
2 chopped onions
3 tbsp. (45 mL) sunflower or canola oil
2 cups (500 mL) coarsely chopped mushrooms
1 tbsp. (15 mL) olive oil
4 cups (1 L) water
2 tbsp. (30 g) butter
2 tbsp. (30 g) flour
½ cup (125 mL) milk (2% or heavier)
nutmeg, salt and pepper to taste

Scrape away the salsify skin with a vegetable peeler, and cut into ½-inch (1.25 cm) lengths. Heat sunflower oil in pan. Add onion. Saute until translucent. Add salsify, cover pan and cook 10 to 15 minutes, stirring occasionally, until fork-tender.

In another pan, braise mushrooms in olive oil until they have given off their liquid. Drain mushrooms, reserving liquid. Add the mushrooms to the salsify and onions. Cover with water, bring to a boil, and then simmer an additional 20 minutes.

In a third saucepan, melt the butter, stir in the flour, and then slowly add the mushroom liquid, followed by the milk. When this mixture begins to thicken, gradually stir in the salsify-onion-mushroom mixture and the seasonings. Once all the ingredients are well-mixed, pour the soup into a blender, and purée until smooth. Reheat slowly just prior to serving.

be sure to leave a few late summer flowers on the plants to set seed for the following summer.

It is possible to harvest salsify after just one growing season, but for really good-sized roots it's advisable to wait until year two, and that way you can enjoy the flowers as well as the root. Salsify should be harvested after the first frosts, as the colder temperatures intensify and sweeten its flavor as well as improving its texture. Roots can also be left in the ground over winter if a mulch is applied to the soil surface, to be harvested the following spring. The flavor of salsify doesn't improve with storage, so the best-tasting roots will always be those that go straight from the garden to the kitchen counter.

The easiest way to prepare salsify is to scrape off the skin with a vegetable peeler, and boil it in salted, acidulated water for 15 to 20 minutes. The roots will discolor quickly once they lose their skin, so get them into the water as quickly as possible. Drain the roots and cut them into rounds. Then, in a frying pan, melt some butter (or use your favorite cooking oil), and add minced garlic, a little citrus zest, and

chopped parsley. Simmer at a low heat until the salsify begins to turn golden brown (5 to 10 minutes). Yum, yum!

Scorzonera

Scorzonera hispanica

IN SPITE OF belonging to different genera, scorzonera and salsify are often treated simultaneously in gardening texts. Certainly, both are members of the Compositae or daisy family, and both are closely related to lettuce, chicory and dandelions. Furthermore, both are employed similarly in the kitchen, and any recipe calling for salsify will be equally good (and perhaps even better) with scorzonera. Be that as it may, scorzonera is a separate genus which comprises at least 150 species, only one of which (*S. hispanica*) is of interest to cottage gardeners.

A perennial vegetable (like asparagus and rhubarb), scorzonera is native to Europe from Portugal to southern Siberia, and is hardy to zones 3 to 4. Like salsify, the young leaves and flowers are edible, but it is for the long, black tapering roots that most vegetable gardeners grow this attractive plant. Bearing golden yellow flowers over a long period, scorzonera is equally at home in the herbaceous borders, and although it is generally considered a short-lived perennial, I have several plants that have been blooming steadily for at least a decade. The foliage of scorzonera is broader than that of salsify, the bright green leaves closely resembling those of yellow foxglove (*Digitalis lutea*), so be sure you don't confuse the two if you're out for a graze.

NAME: Salsify *Tragopogon porrifolius*

HEIGHT: To 5' (1.5 m)

EXPOSURE: Sun

BLOOMING PERIOD: Late spring to autumn

SOIL: Ordinary garden soil with good drainage. Avoid using manure

COMPANIONS: Due to its upright habit, salsify associates well with "floppy" plants such as double creeping buttercup (*Ranunculus repens* 'Pleniflorus') and blue mallow (*Malva sylvestris* 'Primley Blue')

SPECIAL NOTES: The attractive purple flowers usually close at noon

Scorzonera is sometimes marketed as black salsify or black oyster plant. Unfortunately both names are misleading since, like salsify, it doesn't taste like oysters (it has a delicious nutty flavor), and in Europe chefs generally prize scorzonera roots above those of salsify. Scorzonera has a reputation as a gourmet vegetable, perhaps because King Louis XIV of France grew it in great quantities, but this exclusivity is completely groundless. Scorzonera is an easy plant to grow with few disease or pest problems, and any gardener can nurture it successfully.

The seeds should be started the same way as salsify, although you can expect germination rates to be a little lower. Scorzonera also doesn't self-seed readily in colder regions, so stock must be increased in subsequent years either by root division or with new seedlings. Soil requirements for both plants are the same. When grown for the table rather than for show, scorzonera may be harvested after one growing season, though you'll get bigger crops if you leave it in the ground for two years. Roots must be carefully harvested after the first frosts as they are more brittle than those of salsify.

The biggest difference between salsify and scorzonera is in the actual cooking – it is essential that scorzonera be cooked with its black skin intact, to be peeled away after cooking is complete. Most of the flavor of scorzonera lies in the skin, and if it's removed prior to cooking, the result will be insipid at best. The Victorians were great scrubbers of vegetables, and this is the primary reason that scorzonera fell from favor during that era. Bereft of its skin, and boiled to within an inch of its life, this once aristocratic vegetable was reduced to an unappetizing pulpy mush.

There is some debate about how the genus name of scorzonera first arose, but in English records going back as far as 1560, it is usually referred to as viper's grass and was considered an antidote to snake bites. This association with snakes appears to be plausible, since "scorzonera" probably originated from the Spanish *escorzo* or the Old French *scorzon*, both of which mean "serpent." Scorzonera was also believed to be effective in treating smallpox during the Middle Ages. Containing inulin (a polysaccharide), scorzonera is an easily digestible form of carbohydrates for diabetics. Inulin is also responsible for the sweet, nutty flavor of scorzonera, a taste treat that no enthusiastic cottage gardener should deny themselves.

Scorzonera was widely grown throughout the Spanish Empire in the seventeenth century (hence the species name *hispanica*), and from Spain it spread across Europe becoming an important staple vegetable. To this day, scorzonera is available in many European countries either canned (not so good) or frozen (better, but not as good as freshly dug!). Like salsify, named cultivars of scorzonera are practically indistinguishable from wild forms. Sometimes the Belgian cultivar 'Black Giant Russian' (or 'Geante Noir de Russe') is available, and produces roots of exceptional quality.

NAME: Scorzonera *Scorzonera hispanica*

HEIGHT: To 5' (1.5 m)

EXPOSURE: Sun

BLOOMING PERIOD: Summer to early autumn

SOIL: Ordinary to rich garden soil

COMPANIONS: Looks great with ❀ willow blue-star (*Amsonia tabernaemontana*) or blue bugloss (*Anchusa azurea* 'Loddon Royalist')

SPECIAL NOTES: Mature plants may require some staking

Antique Vegetables Suitable for North American Cottage Gardens

Amaranth (*Amaranthus tricolor*) – Annual with colorful foliage, native to tropical Asia; cook the edible leaves and stem tips like spinach.

❧ Asparagus (*Asparagus officinalis*) Perennial, hardy to zones 4–5. Separate male and female plants. Modern cultivars such as 'Mary Washington' and 'Martha Washington' are disease resistant. Taking four years from sowing seed to harvesting crops, it's best to buy established roots. Look out for the heirloom varieties. 'Argenteuil Early' (France, 1885), and 'Conover's Colossal' (New York, 1870).

❧ Beans (some) (*Phaseolus* spp.) Annual. Native varieties of beans include common, lima, runner and tepary types. Most beans are easy to grow and many have very showy flowers. The following varieties are especially suitable for cottage gardens:
'Broad Windsor' (1863) A 'fava' or broad bean, one of the oldest of cultivated plants.
'Canadian Wonder' (1873) A snap bush bean with excellent vigor and hardiness.
'Kentucky Wonder Wax' (1901) A wax pole bean bearing bright yellow pods, good in cool climates.
'Painted Lady' (1855) A runner bean whose flowers have red wings and light pink standards.

❧ Cabbage (*Brassica oleracea*, Capitata group) Annual. Cabbages are part of a close-knit family that includes kale, collards, broccoli, Brussels sprouts

Closely related to beetroot, Swiss chard (Beta vulgaris subsp. cicla) is grown for its colorful, edible leaf petioles (or stalks), which are best prepared steamed or included in stir-fries. The leaves are also edible but should be consumed in moderation as they contain significant amounts of calcium oxalate, which can be toxic if ingested in high quantities.

and cauliflower. Here are few of the older varieties — try mixing them in with some of the newer ones and compare performance and flavor when you harvest.

'Brunswick' (1880) Green, flat "drumhead type" heads up to 6 lbs. (2.5 kg).

'Danish Ballhead' (1887) 6 lb. (2.5 kg) blue-green heads, somewhat bolt-resistant.

'Early Jersey Wakefield' (New Jersey, 1845) Small, pale green 3 lb. (1.25 kg) compact heads.

'Mammoth Red Rock' (1905) Good red-purple color to the core, excellent winter keeper.

Carrot (*Daucus carota* var. *sativus*) Biennial, but grown as an annual. In the wild, carrots come in many different colors (white, yellow, red and purple), and it wasn't until the second half of the nineteenth century that the French developed the standard orange form we recognize today. Like most root crops, carrots like a loose soil; sandy loam is ideal.

'Belgian White' (1863) 9" (22.5 cm) Long white roots, mild flavor with a good crunch.

'Danvers Half Long' (Massachusetts, 1871) 7" (17.5 cm) Long orange roots, stores well.

'Early Scarlet Horn' (Holland, 1610) Stumpy roots up to 6" (15 cm) long, best used when young.

'Topweight' (England, 1750) 11" (27.5 cm) Bright orange root which will over-winter with some protection in most areas, making seed collection the following year an easy task.

Swiss Chard (*Beta vulgaris* subsp. *cicla*) — Annual, native to Europe. Look for cultivar 'Bright Lights' developed in New Zealand and an All America Selections Winner.

❀ Corn (*Zea mays*) Annual. A true native, and it grows better in North America than anywhere else on the globe. The following varieties are known as sweet corn, which is the standard old-fashioned open-pollinated type. Be forewarned, however, that you can't grow the newer sugar-enhanced or super-sweet varieties anywhere nearby — it must be one or the other, or both types will be spoiled (all types of corn are wind-pollinated).

'Catawba' (New York, 1909) White kernels, with ornamental red-hued stalks and leaves.

'Golden Bantam' (Massachusetts, 1902) Before this variety came along, yellow corn was considered little more than cattle-feed. Six-inch (15 cm) ears on 6' (1.8 m) stalks.

'Howling Mob' (Ohio 1905) White-kerneled 8" (20 cm) ears, height to 6' (1.8 m).

'Stowell's Evergreen' (New Jersey, 1848) White-kerneled 9" (22.5 cm) ears, height to 9' (3 m).

Fiddleheads — Ostrich fern (*Matteuccia struthiopteris*) — Perennial fern hardy to zone 3, widely distributed across the northern hemisphere. Not to be confused with the carcinogenic bracken fern (*Pteridium aquilinum*).

Good King Henry (*Chenopodium bonus-henricus*) — Perennial, hardy to zones 4–5, and native to Europe. Introduced to Britain during the Bronze Age. Eventually named after Henry VIII's father, Henry VII who reigned from 1485–1509. The young leaves and shoots are cooked like spinach but taste like asparagus.

❀ Groundnut (*Apios americana*) — Native perennial vine, hardy to zone 4. The tubers were eaten by American Indians and helped to save the pilgrims from starvation during their first winters in New England.

This eclectic combination of asparagus (Asparagus officinalis) and raspberries (Rubus spp.) makes perfect botanical sense: Asparagus shoots are harvested in late spring before the raspberries leaf out. By midsummer, the maturing foliage of the asparagus admits sufficient sunlight to ripen the berries, thereby securing two perennial crops from just one patch of soil.

Lettuce (*Lactuca sativus*) Annual. The basis of any good salad (excepting Greek), lettuce prefers a cool growing season, so it is best planted in early spring. With the onset of hot weather it tends to bolt (flower and set seed), which spoils the flavor. Be sure to sneak in a second late season crop at the end of the summer, to mature before the first frosts.
'Oak Leaf' (18th century) Tolerant of hot weather; look out for the ornamental 'Red Oak Leaf'
'Speckled' (Old Mennonite var.) Ornamental green leaves, flecked with maroon, Bibb-type head.
'Tennis Ball' (1800) Light green leaves that pale to yellow at the base. Thomas Jefferson grew it!
'Tom Thumb' (England, 1830) Miniature butter-head type, each head perfect for a single serving.

Onion (*Allium* spp. and cultivars) All cottage gardeners love onions, not only in their edible form, but also in their important role as an ornamental. Too few people know that to leave a few leeks in your garden for a second year will produce gorgeous blooms, good enough to rival any *Allium giganteum*. Here are a few suggestions to steer you in the right direction.
'Red Wethersfield' (*A. cepa*, Cepa group) (Connecticut, 1800) Purple skin with white flesh, well-suited to northern gardeners.
Welsh Onion (*A. fistulosum*) Perennial to zones 4–5. Used like scallions, with attractive flowers.
Egyptian Onion (*A. cepa*, Proliferum group) Perennial to zone 5. Garden sculpture for free! These onions not only form underground bulbs, but they also form bulblets on the top of each flowering stalk. Very Dr. Seuss.
Shallots (*A. cepa*, Aggregatum group) Look for 'Odetta's White Shallot' (Kansas, 1900).

Garden Orach (*Atriplex hortensis*) — Self-seeding annual, native to Europe and tolerant of saline soils. Use the leaves; again the taste is very like spinach but less bitter.

Peas (*Pisum sativum*) Peas are another vegetable that prefer the cool temperatures of spring and early summer. Sow seeds as soon as the ground can be worked early in the year. Most of the old pea varieties are semi-dwarf, seldom reaching more than 3' (90 cm) in height. Here's an excellent opportunity to experiment with some "peastick teepees," made up of discarded shrub and tree prunings, wired together at the top.
'Champion of England' (1846) Introduced to North America in 1849; rich flavor on short plants
'Lincoln' (1908) Cream-colored peas on semi-dwarf plants, good choice for northern gardens.
'Stratagem' (England, 1879) Introduced to North America in 1883, having just received two RHS awards. Excellent choice for the Northwest.
'Thomas Laxton' (England, 1898) Introduced to North America in 1900, it's still popular and widely available today. Semi-dwarf.

Peppers (*Capsicum annuum*) Native to the warmest regions of the Americas, the archaeologists assure us that peppers have been consumed since 7,000 BC. Definitely a warm-season crop, don't plant peppers until it's safe for the tomatoes. Peppers like to be well-nourished and well-watered to produce the best crops.
'Arledge Hot' (Louisiana) Tabasco-type pepper, 4" (10 cm) long, very hot. Performs well in northern regions.
'Chiltepine' (Texas) The only hot pepper that grows wild within the borders of the United States. Behaves as a perennial if over-wintered indoors. Deliciously hot.
'Karlo' (Romania) Compact plants produce 4"

(20 cm) long peppers that mature from yellow to red. Semi-hot, semi-sweet, and totally tasty.
'Sweet Banana' (Hungary, 1941) Thick flesh with a sweet, mild taste. Begs to be stuffed with ricotta cheese, and then breaded and deep-fried or baked in a moderate oven. Blissful!

Rampion (*Campanula rapunculus*) – Biennial, and native to Europe with white to light blue bell-shaped flowers. Once a popular edible root, the species is named after the Brothers Grimm fairy tale *Rapunzel*, in which it features. Not to be confused with the weedy creeping bellflower (*Campanula rapunculoides*).

Skirret (*Sium sisarum*) – Perennial, and native to Eurasia, bearing white umbelliferous (attracts beneficial insects) flowers. A popular Elizabethan root vegetable, hardy to zones 5–6.

Tomato (*Lycopersicon lycopersicum*) Tomatoes rank as North America's number one home garden crop, and like corn, it grows best in North America. Heat, rich soil, regular watering, and you have it made. Here are my six favorite heirloom tomato varieties.
'Burbank' (California, 1915) Developed by the celebrated American naturalist and plant breeder, Luther Burbank (1849–1926) and the only tomato he would allow to bear his name. Hardy and disease resistant with medium-sized red fruit; great flavor.
'Gardener's Delight' (England, mid-1800's) Prolific plants bear cherry-sized tomatoes, the best I've ever tasted. Bright red, crack-resistant fruit.
'Marmande' (France, 1920s) Eight-ounce (225 g) irregularly shaped scarlet fruits are most French chefs' choice for dishes requiring sliced tomatoes. Fabulous flavor with a firm, meaty flesh.
'Brandywine' (USA Amish, 1885) Deep pink skin, somewhat prone to radial cracking, but mouth-

*The enduring appeal of the cottage garden style is succinctly summed up in garden consultant Ellen Eisenberg's coupling of blue fleabane (*Erigeron spp.*) with tomato (*Lycopersicon lycopersicum*).*

watering nonetheless. Indeterminate plants bear fruit up to 2 lbs. (1 kg).
'Oxheart' (USA, 1925) The strange shape of this tomato results from a natural gene mutation. Seven-ounce (200 g) rose-colored fruit is meaty and firm with a mild flavor, and few seeds.
'Yellow Pear' (1805) Another case of "If I could only grow one tomato . . ." Probably dating as far back as 1600, vines are vigorous, and if a few over-ripe fruits are left on the soil surface, they will invariably produce seedlings the following season, in fact, acting like a hardy self-seeding annual. Disease-resistant plants bear hundreds of one-ounce (28 g) pale yellow pear-shaped fruit that look as ornamental in a pasta or salad as they do in the garden.

CHAPTER EIGHT

Pulling It All Together

Now that we've had a good look at some of the plants you'll be installing in your North American cottage garden, let's recap what you need to remember before you put your spade to soil.

Evaluate What You've Got

The first consideration will be to review the existing permanent structures and plant material on your property. Rather than trying to hide garden sheds and garages, "tart them up" with climbing vines, trellises and window boxes. Soften hard surfaces and edges by placing different-sized containers around them, filled with colorful annuals, tender bulbs, herbs and veg-etables. Add a rustic bench or two. When planting in areas where mature trees exist, be sure to choose plants that will tolerate dry, shady, nutrient-poor conditions. Deciduous trees may be pruned or "limbed-up" — that is, the lower branches are removed to increase light levels and air circulation around the base of the tree.

*Self-seeding annuals like love-in-a-mist (*Nigella damascena*) and cosmos (*Cosmos bipinnatus, pictured here*) are indispensable for adding long-lasting color to a primarily perennial border. Best of all, their diaphanous framework doesn't tie up much real estate, and concentrated planting patterns dispense with the need for staking.*

Plan the Paths

Next, map out (in your head, at least!), where the paths are to be located, and what they are to be constructed of. Remember to make them wide enough that a wheelbarrow can pass through effortlessly, and also ensure that they provide ready access to all sections of the garden for easy weeding and general maintenance. If you do decide to keep a patch or two of lawn, attempt to place the paths in areas that will provide the best view of the garden. This is also a good time to think about where vertical structures (arbors, trellises, arches) will add the most impact. Placing these upright structures in sunny rather than shady areas will give you a much wider choice of suitable plant material. If you are considering adding a birdbath or a sundial to augment these upright structures, remember that the watchword is "simplicity."

Your House

Many North American homeowners worry that their post-war houses are unsuitable structures to encompass with a cottage garden. Nothing could be farther from the truth. I live in a bungalow that was constructed in 1956, hardly ideal, but you can work with what you have! Adding a climbing Japanese hydrangea-vine (*Schizophragma hydrangeoides*), American wisteria (*Wisteria frutescens*) or perhaps some Boston ivy (*Parthenocissus tricuspidata*) will gradually camouflage your house's exterior, so that soon, it disappears into little more than windows, doors and a roof. In addition, once your cottage garden hits its stride, no one is going to be looking at your house anyway! Visually, the primary function of your residence will be to "ground" the garden, serving to emphasize the scale of the property as a whole, and little else.

Design

You probably know by now that most "modern" design principles aren't relevant to a "classic cottage garden look." Nevertheless, most gardeners will want to take certain considerations into account: plant height, flowering sequences, leaf texture, and color combinations. Plants with distinctive characteristics (size, leaf texture, flower color) require careful positioning in a garden of any kind. I find Jerusalem Cross (*Lychnis chalcedonica*) a difficult plant to place, and I have a great deal of it, having grown some from seed over a decade ago. One of the truly vermilion-hued plants, it needs to be isolated from anything pink — the two colors side-by-side are too horrible to contemplate. Many of these decisions will, in the end, come down to basic personal preference, and this is as it should be.

Maintenance

Although a well-constructed cottage garden should be essentially low maintenance (of necessity, I abandon my garden on a regular basis from the beginning of May until the end of June), some regular care will be needed, especially during the first three years, while it's becoming established. Before plants begin to really fill in, weeding will be a regular chore. Some self-seeding plants will need thinning or deadheading to keep them under control, and like it or not, some plants (delphiniums, for sure) will require staking. Again, the best approach is a relaxed one. If I don't get around to staking all the peonies before they bloom, it provides me with a great excuse to cut some flowers for the house. Plants that are completely floppy are generally not attractive, but a casual, blowsy look is, so don't become obsessed with the notion of maintaining a totally tidy garden.

A classic cottage garden vista like this is certainly within your grasp, providing you remember to plant densely (but never in straight lines), keep garden hardware and ornamentation to a minimum, and strive for drifts of color. Sequence of bloom is also an important consideration, so you should aim to be "in flower" from the first winter aconite (Eranthis hyemalis) to the last Japanese anemone (Anemone x hybrida).

The main objective is to enjoy the garden's bounty, and not to get overly involved with making every corner look perfectly manicured. Cut a few flowers, gather some herbs, and harvest some vegetables. Attempt a few new recipes, and expand your culinary horizons. Take the time to give every new blossom a really good sniff. Photograph your garden's progress on a regular basis — it's an excellent way to see just how far you've come, and to measure how far you still have to go.

Above all, be good to your soil, and remember that you aren't the only one who ever has used it, nor are you the only one who ever will use it. Treat it as a living organism, respect it, nurture it, and feed it. It will reward you richly. Hand in hand with healthy soil, you can maintain the venerable old cottage garden style on your own property, bringing it kicking and screaming into the new millennium, and then passing it on to the next generation as so many cottage gardeners have done in the past. It's a rich legacy, and it's imploring you to become a part of it.

COTTAGE GARDENS
OF THE FUTURE

In North America the future of cottage gardens seems assured. Never before have we had such a large number of plants from which to choose. As cottage gardens evolve in different regions of the continent they will inevitably assume certain individual characteristics, primarily reflecting their climatic conditions. This is as it should be, and certainly anyone can tell at a glance the difference between a cottage garden in Scotland as opposed to one in Cornwall. Why then should a cottage garden in Washington State look like one in Nova Scotia? This contrast is to be celebrated rather than eschewed.

The other point that all cottage gardeners must bear in mind is something one of my university professors emphasized in his first lecture of my first semester: "You'll never have all the answers!" Horticulture by its very nature is always changing, evolving and moving forward. New discoveries are constantly being made, and no one person can be an expert in every area of such a sprawling discipline. In other words, never be afraid to say "I don't know," or "I've never heard of that." Asking questions is the only sure path to enlightenment.

Joining a local horticulture group or becoming a member of a plant society is a good way to start making contacts. If you have Internet capability, you're laughing. You could join either the American or English Cottage Garden Societies, or both. If you want to specialize in a particular genus, why not get some information about the American Penstemon Society or the English Delphinium Society? Many seed catalogs are also now online and can provide hours of blissful browsing, especially if you're looking for something hard to find. Even if you aren't online, all these organizations still happily accept letters by post.

Whatever route you decide to take, the first step will always be to go outside and start digging. Happy cottage gardening!

Plant and Catalog Source List

CANADA

Campberry Farm
R.R. 1
Niagara-on-the-Lake, ON
L0S 1J0
TEL: (905) 262-4927
Specializing in hardy and productive nut
trees.

Florabunda Seeds
P.O. Box 3
Indian River, ON
K0L 2B0
TEL: (705) 295-6440
FAX: (705) 295-4035
E-MAIL: contact@florabundaseeds.com
WEB SITE: www.florabundaseeds.com
Dedicated to preserving old flower vari-
eties, with special emphasis on cottage
garden plants.

Fragrant Flora
3741 Sunshine Coast Highway
R.R. 5, Site 21, C 11
Gibsons, BC
V0N 1V0
TEL & FAX: (604) 885-6142
E-MAIL: fragrant_flora@sunshine.net
A comprehensive listing of fragrant
plants, some rare.

Horticulture Indigo
80 route 116
Ulverton, QC
J0B 2B0
TEL: (819) 826-3314
FAX: (819) 826-1011
E-MAIL: indigo@microtec.net
Native flora of Quebec, including
groundnut (*Apois americana*). Catalog in
French and botanical Latin.

Martin & Kraus
P.O. Box 12
1191 Centre Road
Carlisle, ON
L0R 1H0
TEL: (905) 689-0230
FAX: (905) 689-1358
WEB SITE: www.gardenrose.com
Good selection of shrub, Explorer and
Parkland roses.

Pickering Nurseries
670 Kingston Road
Pickering, ON
L1V 1A6
TEL: (905) 839-2111
FAX: (905) 839-4807
A huge selection of old and rare roses.
Shipped bareroot, autumn and spring.

Richters Herbs
357 Highway 47
Goodwood, ON
L0C 1A0
TEL: (905) 640-6677
FAX: (905) 640-6641
E-MAIL: orderdesk@richters.com
WEB SITE: www.richters.com
Probably the largest collection of herbs
you'll ever see in one place. Plants and
seed.

Seeds of Distinction
P.O. Box 86
Station A Etobicoke
Toronto, ON
M9C 4V2
TEL: (416) 255-3060
FAX: (888) 327-9193
E-MAIL: sod@interlog.com
WEB SITE: www.seedsofdistinction.com
First-class selection of rare and unusual
flower seeds.

Vesey's Seeds
P.O. Box 9000
Charlottetown, PE
C1A 8K6
TEL: (800) 363-7333
FAX: (800) 686-0329
E-MAIL: order@veseys.com
WEB SITE: www.veseys.com
Large selection of flower and vegetable
seeds, many well-adapted to shorter
growing seasons.

William Dam Seeds
P.O. Box 8400
Dundas, ON
L9H 6M1
TEL: (905) 628-6641
FAX: (905) 627-1729
E-MAIL: willdam@sympatico.ca
Good selection of old-fashioned flower
and vegetable seed.

UNITED STATES

Abundant Life Seed Foundation
P.O. Box 772
Port Townsend, WA
98368
TEL: (360) 385-5660
FAX: (360) 385-7455
E-MAIL: abundant@olypen.com
A non-profit organization dedicated to
the preservation of genetic diversity.

D. V. Burrell Seed Growers
P.O. Box 150
405 North Main Street
Rocky Ford, CO
81067
TEL: (719) 254-3318
FAX: (719) 254-3319
Large selection of vegetable seeds; some
flowers.

The Gourmet Gardener
8650 College Boulevard
Overland Park, KS
66210-1806
TEL: (913) 345-0490
FAX: (913) 451-2443
WEB SITE: www.gourmetgardener.com
Great selection of edible flowers and
gourmet vegetables, some heirloom.

Heirloom Seeds
P.O. Box 245
W. Elizabeth, PA
15088-0245
WEB SITE: www.heirloomseeds.com
Non-hybrid, open-pollinated vegetables, herbs and flowers.

Heronswood Nursery
7530 NE 288th Street
Kingston, WA
98346
TEL: (360) 297-4172
FAX: (360) 297-8321
E-MAIL: heronswood@silverlink.net
WEB SITE: www.heronswood.com
The catalog is a massive work, and well worth the $5 (U.S.). Perfect for "genus collectors."

Johnny's Selected Seeds
1 Foss Hill Road
R.R. 1, P.O. Box 2580
Albion, ME
04910-9731
TEL: (207) 437-4301
FAX: (207) 437-2165
E-MAIL: staff@johnnyseeds.com
WEB SITE: www.johnnyseeds.com
Very good general selection—especially useful is the cultural information given at the beginning of each entry.

Park Seed
1 Parkton Avenue
Greenwood, SC
29647-0001
TEL: (800) 845-3369
FAX: (864) 941-4206
E-MAIL: info@parkseed.com
WEB SITE: www.parkseed.com
Around since 1868; depend on finding all your old favorites as well as brand-new introductions.

Prairie Nursery
P.O. Box 306
Westfield, WI
53964-0306
TEL: (800) 476-9453
FAX: (608) 476-2741
E-MAIL:
customerservice@prairienursery.com
WEB SITE: www.prairienursery.com

Specializing in native prairie species; the "Planning Information" section is invaluable.

Seeds of Change
P.O. Box 15700
Santa Fe, NM
87506-5700
TEL: (888) 762-7333
FAX: (888) 329-4762
E-MAIL: gardener@seedsofchange.com
WEB SITE: www.seedsofchange.com
All seed is organically produced, and only open-pollinated varieties are listed.

Select Seeds Antique Flowers
180 Stickney Hill Road
Union, CT
06076-4617
TEL: (860) 684-9310
FAX: (800) 653-3304
E-MAIL: info@selectseeds.com
WEB SITE: www.selectseeds.com
A great source for old-fashioned plants and seeds that even sports a phonetic guide to botanical pronunciation!

OTHER

Chiltern Seeds
Bortree Stile
Ulverston, Cumbria
England LA12 7PB
TEL: + (44) 01229 581137
FAX: + (44) 01229 584549
E-MAIL:
chilternseeds@compuserve.com
Very likely the largest seed catalog in print, Chiltern Seeds caters to North American customers without batting an eye.

Natural Insect Control
R.R. 2
Stevensville, ON
L0S 1S0
TEL: (905) 382-2904
FAX: (905) 382-4418
E-MAIL: nic@niagara.com
WEB SITE:
www.natural-insect-control.com
Beneficial insects by mail as well as other types of "earth friendly" products.

SOCIETIES

The Cottage Garden Society (UK)
For membership information contact:
Clive Lane, Esq.
Hurstfield House (CGS)
244 Edleston Road
Crewe, Cheshire
England CW2 7EJ
WEB SITE:
www.alfresco.demon.co.uk/cgs/index.html

The North American Cottage Garden Society
This society is re-grouping and should be up and running by 2000.
For membership information contact:
Ms. Denis Garrett
NACGS Membership Secretary
2765 Old Sams Creek Road
Pegram, TN
37143

The Royal Horticultural Society
For membership information contact:
Membership Secretary
P.O. Box 313
80 Vincent Square
London
England SW1P 2PE
WEB SITE: www.rhs.org.uk/

The Internet Directory for Botany
(Courtesy of the Finnish Museum of Natural History)
If it's plant societies you're after, here's the place to start. A massive site, arranged both by location and plant genus. International, but with plenty of North American contacts.
WEB SITE:
www.sysbot.gu.se/mirrors/idb/botsoc/.html

An allied Canadian botanical site can be found at:
www.botany.net/
or an American one at:
www.botany.org/

Index